The leadership tide is constantly changing, and Jonathan does a great job outlining what it's going to take to lead as a next generation leader going forward. One of the big questions today is transitioning leadership from one generation to the next. *Next Up* meets that challenge head-on with a practical plan you can put into practice!

BRAD LOMENICK
Author of *The Catalyst Leader*, president and lead visionary of Catalyst

Passing the leadership baton is no easy task, but receiving it is an even more daunting responsibility. With practical yet profound wisdom, Jonathan Pearson gives young leaders such necessary tools to face this challenge and steward their influence with grace and excellence.

PETE WILSON
Pastor of Cross Point Church, author of *Plan B* and *Let Hope In*

Jonathan's book takes me back to my early days as a leader— those days of great ambition, boundless zeal, and no clue what I was really doing. With uncompromising insight, Jonathan emphasizes the unglamorous traits—honor, humility, patience— that make real leaders out of what might have been just a flash in the pan. Whether you're fresh out of the gate or in the home stretch, this is the leadership book you need to run your race strong.

SCOTT WILLIAMS
Church growth/le   xt
Level Solutions, a   3ig

The leadership pipeline in most organizations and churches is thin. In many cases, we have neglected the process of leadership development. But a new crew of leadership is on the rise. Will they be ready? Jonathan bravely challenges his younger leader peers to step up to the plate and seize their day. This is a helpful and engaging book for all generations preparing for who is "Next Up."

RON EDMONDSON
Blogger at RonEdmondson.com, senior pastor of
Immanuel Baptist Church in Lexington, Kentucky

As a young leader imagining the future of our organization, *Next Up* has been a literal handbook.

BLAINE HOGAN
Creative director at Willow Creek Community Church

Jonathan is one of the brightest young leaders I know. He also lives out what it means to honor the past and press toward the future as a young leader. Every young leader should read this work!

SHAWN LOVEJOY
Lead pastor of Mountain Lake Church, author of *The Measure of Our Success: An Impassioned Plea to Pastors*

The youngest generation of leaders has often been unfairly generalized as spoiled and selfish. Jonathan Pearson throws light on a better way to lead in the middle of today's hurricane of cultural change. His message is timely yet rooted in timeless truth, and our age needs stronger roots to bear fresh fruit. A generation yet to have their chance depends on it.

BRANDON COX
Pastor of Grace Hills Church in Bentonville, Arkansas, author of *Rewired*

When I see Jonathan at a distance or up close, he represents what Christ taught us with faith, hope and love. In *Next Up*, he communicates that kind of leadership in a real, relevant and engaging way.

> WAYNE ELSEY
> Founder of Soles4Souls

Jonathan issues a bold call to young leaders, one that, if followed, will prepare them well as the next generation of leadership. I have seen firsthand how the negative traits he addresses can keep leaders from reaching their full potential. And on the flip side, I have seen leaders soar as they develop consistency, passion, humility, and patience. Jonathan's book is a much-needed resource for any young leader desiring to lead well.

> JUSTIN LATHROP
> Founder of YoungPastors.com

Jonathan Pearson's *Next Up* is bringing to front and center characteristics and values that should grab the hearts and minds of millennials everywhere. The choice to move forward, make changes, and commit to sustainable personal leadership development and progress has been a continuous challenge and theme for my thirty-five years of working and ministering to college age students. Pearson provides students serious about personal and professional growth a clear, concise framework for seizing the leadership opportunities God has placed in their path. If achieving success navigating the challenges of the 21st century is a goal you share, then I highly recommend that millennials, and those who mentor them, give *Next Up* full attention.

> DR. RICK BREWER
> Vice president of Student Affairs and Athletics,
> Charleston Southern University

If you're in leadership at any level, whether inside the church or in the secular world, this book will serve you well. For older leaders, this is a vital read to help prepare the next generation of leadership. For younger leaders, this is vital to help prepare them if God sees fit for them to continue to lead at an increasingly higher level.

The work that Jonathan has done will serve you well, and help prepare you for the road that God has ahead of you. You owe it to your organization to process the concepts here. If you want to be a responsible leader, read this book.

BEN REED
Small groups pastor of Long Hollow, author of *Starting Small: The Ultimate Small Group Blueprint*

I love young, sharp, aggressive leaders. There is nothing more exciting than turning one of these young lions loose, but we often fail them in forgetting that great leadership happens when opportunity meets with preparation. Jonathan's book stands out as the perfect tool to help ensure the next generation is prepped and ready to pick up the leadership torch in your church or organization.

TODD ADKINS
Director of Leadership, Lifeway Christian Resources

NEXT UP

8 SHIFTS
GREAT YOUNG
LEADERS MAKE

JONATHAN PEARSON

Moody Publishers

CHICAGO

Edited by Bailey Utecht
Cover design: Connie Gabbert Design
Interior design: Ragont Design

Library of Congress Cataloging-in-Publication Data

Pearson, Jonathan, 1986-
Next up : 8 shifts great young leaders make / Jonathan Pearson.
pages cm
Summary: "There are 8 key attitude and action shifts that every great leader makes. From entitlement to honor. From passive to passionate. From unreliable to consistent. Are you willing to make these shifts and be ready when the "next up" call comes? The Millennial Generation is poised to do something. We have an opportunity to learn, grow, ask for help, and lead honorably into the future. Or...we also have the potential to passively wait, feeling entitled for the keys to eventually be given to us-but we can do better than that! Let's take the initiative and rise to the challenge. The future will be filled with leadership transitions at not only the highest levels in businesses, churches, and organizations all over the world, but also at regular, everyday places. Who will be ready to lead existing movements, groups, and causes? Or who will be ready to start the new ones? Using practical, biblical, and contemporary examples and lessons this book will help existing and burgeoning leaders pinpoint the areas of their lives where they still need to make the shift and learn to lead more effectively"-- Provided by publisher.
Includes bibliographical references.
ISBN 978-0-8024-1171-6 (paperback)
1. Leadership--Religious aspects--Christianity. 2. Career development. I. Title.
HD57.7.P4293 2014
658.4'092--dc23
2014001985

We hope you enjoy this book from Moody Publishers. Our goal is to provide high-quality, thought-provoking books and products that connect truth to your real needs and challenges. For more information on other books and products written and produced from a biblical perspective, go to www.moodypublishers.com or write to:

Moody Publishers
820 N. LaSalle Boulevard
Chicago, IL 60610

1 3 5 7 9 10 8 6 4 2

Printed in the United States of America

CONTENTS

Foreword   9

Shift Ahead   13

#1 – From *Entitlement* to Honor   23

#2 – From *Unreliable* to Consistent   33

#3 – From *Dissension* to Cooperation   45

#4 – From *Conformity* to Integrity   55

#5 – From *Pride* to Humility   69

#6 – From *Passive* to Passionate   79

#7 – From *Selfishness* to Love   93

#8 – From *Premature* to Patient   107

Make the Shift and Go   117

Notes   123

Dedication & Acknowledgments   125

FOREWORD

" . . . Everything the Lord has said we will do."
—Exodus 24:3

My first real job was selling shoes on Saturdays in a little store on Main Street. It was owned by an older God-loving couple who agreed, at the urging of a friend, to give me a part-time job while still in high school. I was only fifteen, but I always wanted to be a "businessman" so I immediately spotted some "deficiencies" in this small operation that I felt needed to be recognized by the owners.

I presented my groundbreaking, money-making ideas with great confidence thinking no one could miss these. Well, you can imagine how that turned out. My ideas were dismissed and disregarded, not because of their lack of value, but for the source from which they came . . . a fifteen-year-old boy on his first job.

I've had many jobs since then, most of which left me unfulfilled and lacking a sense of accomplishment. But I never forgot that feeling of being young, aggressive, loyal, and creative, and at the same time not being taken seriously. I think this "old school" mindset is still in place in many of our churches and organizations. The ideas and input of those who are much younger are too easily rejected or not given the weight they deserve. Young people's ideas are kept in the queue of advancement too long for fear that lack of experience will produce less than stellar results. Any organization that fails to see the value of the next generation of leaders are . . . well, failing.

I planted a church in my hometown of Orangeburg, South Carolina, seventeen years ago. It's a great town, but one that lacks the depth of skilled leaders enjoyed by cities of greater population. But I know God is moving in what seems to be the desolate places. He is raising up the next generation of leaders to serve His church with faith and courage. They have developed skills that will serve His kingdom well when it's time for them to take their place as the senior leaders in the coming years.

Jonathan came to our church in 2010. When he came, I didn't guarantee him a job, a salary, or even a title! All I told him was that if he felt God was leading him to be a pastor at our church, I'd have him a desk. He showed up a couple of weeks later—ready to work for free.

To this day, I'm still thankful Jonathan and his wife, Melissa, chose to step out in faith and join the move of God here. Since that step of obedience, Jonathan has gained influence and been given a ton of different projects, tasks, and opportunities. I've seen Jonathan meet all of them with flying colors.

The ideas Jonathan outlines in this book aren't ones he's simply read or heard and then did a great job at word-smithing to gain the eye of a publisher. I've seen these principles practiced first and then written from a perspective of discovery. As he looked to see what principles guided him to be successful at such a young age, he wanted to share them with other great leaders. Those are outlined in *Next Up*.

Young leaders and senior leaders alike will be glad they read this book. The truth is, whether we like to admit it or not, many of us senior and experienced leaders are coming into the fourth quarter of our leadership. We have to begin thinking now about the people to whom we're going to give the ball as we step aside so a younger generation can take the leadership reins of our churches, businesses, and organizations.

If you're a young leader, the next leader may be you if you're willing to make some key changes now so you'll be ready when that call comes. I can't think of a better and more qualified person to speak to the millennial generation about sound and biblical leadership principles than Jonathan.

The remainder of this book will be an incredible tool for students, experienced leaders, and young leaders alike. It will challenge you to face your shortcomings head-on. You'll be able to come back to this for years and even use it as a handbook to train young leaders to make a valuable impact in your organization.

From all of us "experienced" leaders, we'd like for you to read this book and practice what it outlines. We need you to be next up.

ARTIE DAVIS, Lead Pastor, Cornerstone Community
Church, Orangeburg, South Carolina
Director, The Sticks Network and The Sticks Group
Author, *Craveable: The Irresistable Jesus in Me*

SHIFT AHEAD

I graduated from college on December 13, 2008, and got married that following Saturday. Just five days before Christmas, Melissa and I said "I do" and left out for a quick honeymoon before Christmas day.

A couple days after Christmas with my family, we drove to our new home that both of us had yet to spend a night in and began to sort through wedding gifts and the stacks of boxes yet to be unpacked. It was a great little house. The church I was working for at the time agreed to let us stay there as part of our package for serving. It was on a long road in a small Southern town. It was one of those quiet settings that you usually see in movies. You know, the one where a dirt road runs in front of the house and the nearest neighbor is a quarter of a mile down the street.

Our first night in our new home, Melissa and I were relaxing on our sofa in the living room after a long day of travel and unpacking. We were in the middle of a movie when we heard it! It sounded like someone was coming through the front door. We both jumped to our feet and stared at each other. I had no clue what to do. The only thought I had went something like, "This is my new wife. I'm the man. I have to protect my domain!" I couldn't remember everything the preacher had asked us to say in our vows, but I was confident protecting her was in there somewhere.

So, like any good husband, I hurried Melissa to the bedroom, told her to get under the bed, and grabbed my never-before-shot-by-me shotgun.

Nothing.

I waited for a few seconds . . .

Nothing.

I flipped on the front porch light and looked out of the peep-hole . . .

Nothing.

I opened up the door sure I was going to find someone in the bushes . . .

Nothing.

Finally, I locked the door and went to get Melissa out from under the bed. After looking around for a few minutes, we noticed that a few of my baseball hats had fallen from a shelf that we had against a wall in the living room. Apparently, the sound of the hats hitting the wall and then the floor made it sound like someone was coming into my domain and messing with us.

THE ALARM HAS SOUNDED

Why did I react so suddenly and drastically when Melissa and I heard the sound near our door? It was because I was alarmed. Even more than that, I reacted because I felt like something I cared about was in harm's way. I reacted so dramatically because I knew that someone had to do something, and I was the man to do the job. I was the best option in that moment to protect and take care of my house and my wife. That night sitting on the couch, the alarm went off and I reacted the best way I knew how. That's what we do when we hear alarms; we move.

That's where we are as a generation. The alarm has sounded and we have to react. We are sitting at the threshold of a leadership change and we have to respond. Without us taking action and making the right changes now so that we can be ready to take the baton, we'll see the organizations, churches, and businesses that were started years ago with such passion and vigor become nothing more than a remnant in the timeline of society. We have to take action. We have to wake up.

ARE YOU NEXT UP?

The previous generation started many organizations, businesses, and projects. They began those they believed the world needed and they succeeded in doing so. Some great discoveries, ideas, churches, theories, and other undertakings have been developed as a result of these needs. Those innovators, though, are moving into the fourth quarter of their leadership. In the meantime, the forward-thinking ones are looking to hand off the ball to a new generation. Aging senior pastors are looking for the right person to take their place. Will you be that next generation leader?

THAT'S WHAT we do when we hear alarms, we move.

If so, you'll have to grasp ideas, concepts, and behaviors that aren't typical with our generation. If you're going to be the one who moves ahead of the pack and the one whom senior leaders look to hand the reins to, you are going to have to make some shifts in your attitude, your character, and your thinking. You're going to have to make some bold shifts if you're going to be the one who moves the organization you love ahead. If you're going to be the one who is blessed to get to the next level in leadership, you'll have to shift your thinking and begin thinking like someone worthy to be trusted with a flourishing organization.

Don't get me wrong; I'm not saying that you can't be you. You are definitely going to have to be your unique self. You are going to have to discover the gifts God has put inside you and use them. You can't be your predecessor. The worst thing you could do would be to step outside of who you really are in order to get ahead. First Peter 4:10 gives us some instruction about using our gifts when it says, "Each of you should use whatever gift *you have received* to serve others, as faithful stewards of God's grace in its various forms" (emphasis mine). You have to operate in those God-given gifts and work toward sharpening those gifts as God gives you opportunities.

Your unique personality, your God-given gifts, and a few attitude and mind shifts will be the things that propel you forward to take the reins.

YOU CAN HELP

As a child, I admired my dad. I loved everything about him. Everything Dad did, I wanted to do just like him. I wanted to be a part of whatever he was doing. I watched my dad cut grass from the time I can remember being able to look out a window. I'd watch him outside my bedroom window as a child and dream about cutting grass. As I was growing up, my dad owned a pretty large lawn-maintenance business. He had big equipment that always piqued my interest as a boy. I always wanted to help him and go to the job sites to use the equipment.

So I watched him. It wasn't because I liked being outside or liked seeing his big lawn mower in action—although those were definitely cool too. No, I wanted to help Dad cut grass because it was him doing it. There was no greater feeling as a boy than knowing I was old enough and skilled enough to help my dad with something.

I was about fifteen years old when my dad began to let me go cut grass with him at some of his bigger jobs. It was such a great feeling to know I was good enough to help him. Knowing he needed me to help him with his work and that I was contributing to the family always gave me a fulfillment I never fully understood until I got married and began providing for my family.

We all want to be wanted. We have an innate desire to have other people want us and value us. It's not by mistake that you and I want to feel wanted. That desire to be needed is placed there by a God who wants us to feel love and validation from Him. It's placed there so we can feel

> **YOUR UNIQUE personality, your God-given gifts, and a few attitude and mind shifts will be the things that propel you forward to take the reins.**

and know how much He loves and sacrificed for us.

If you're reading this and thinking, "There's no way I can be next," you're wrong. Sure, God may not call you to take the reins where you are, but you have the potential inside of you to make waves in our generation and in your world. You have inside of you the ability to help the greatest Dad of them all, in what He considers the greatest mission. You have the potential inside of you to help grow the kingdom of God in miraculous and sensational ways.

WANTED: IMPERFECT PEOPLE

Do you remember the story in Luke 5 when Jesus called Peter to be His disciple? Jesus was teaching some people by the lake one day when the crowd began to grow. The crowd grew so much they began to get close to Jesus. Not wanting to go for a swim or stop the crowd from gathering, Jesus hopped in one of the boats He happened to see by the side of the lake. The boat Jesus sort of hijacked and began teaching from just happened to be Peter's (still Simon at the time). When Jesus was done teaching, He turned to Peter and asked Peter to take the boat out into deeper water and try his hand at fishing one more time for the day. Now, keep in mind this is what Peter did for a living. Peter's livelihood was dependent upon him knowing how to fish. Peter wasn't just a weekend fisherman with a cane pole. He had already had a long night at work and had caught nothing, not even a cold. So Jesus asking Peter to try this again didn't seem right. After some arguing, though, Peter agrees to listen to Jesus and take the boat out a little farther into the water.

After Peter and Jesus arrive in deeper waters, you know what Peter has to be thinking: "This guy is a great teacher, but He's about to learn that ol' Pete knows what he's talking about when it comes to fishing." But what happened when Peter reluctantly threw his net out into the water? Something big! The Bible gives a beautiful description of the scene in Luke 5:6 when it says, "They caught such a large number of fish that their nets began to break." Can you imagine the look on Peter's face and the thoughts going through his head? Peter had no answer for all of the fish they caught. All Peter knew to do when he got the fish into the boat was to fall at the feet of Jesus.

I can imagine the tears in Peter's eyes as he looked up at Jesus.

Peter had to feel so messed up and full of faults. Peter, in the presence of the miracle-working Jesus, must have thought he had nothing good to offer. He had to have felt so dirty and screwed up. That is, until Jesus looks down at him in Luke 5:10 and says, "Don't be afraid; from now on you will fish for people." In that moment, Peter had significance. He had something to live for beyond his everyday life. In that moment, Peter experienced a big shift in his attitude, his calling, and his purpose. In fact, the very next verse in Luke 5 says that Peter and the gang left everything to follow Jesus.

Jesus would use Peter for the rest of his life. In fact, if it hadn't been for Peter and his venture from inconsequential to eternally significant, the early church would have looked a lot different. Jesus gives significance. You are significant.

THE INFORMATION AGE

I'll never forget what I was doing the day the Sandy Hook Elementary School shooting took place. I woke up that morning, had a cup of coffee, spent my daily time with God, and started to go through the usual browsing of my apps on my iPad. I opened up Twitter and started reading about a shooting that took place somewhere in Connecticut. Not having a clue about the news before a search of Twitter, I immediately began to search around to find out exactly what happened. Within minutes of the shooting, I had a pretty good grasp of the happenings some eight hundred miles from my South Carolina home.

> IT'S A LOUD world. We're constantly bombarded with the noise of culture.

That's the world we live in. You and I, our generation, are

growing up and living in a world where information, news, and ideas are everywhere we turn. No longer do we have to wait until the next morning's paper to read about the news or wait until five o'clock and turn on our local news broadcast to find out what's happening in the world around us. No longer do we have to look up news or statistics in a book to find the information we want. We are literally connected at all times. We're connected to the news, to resources, and to each other like never before.

We're constantly bombarded with the noise of culture, but it doesn't have to be a bad thing and muddy our minds. It can be a good thing that allows us to grow, to learn, and to have an impact on the world around us. In fact, some of this noise is necessary information that can put us well ahead of the curve of the past.

There's a natural inclination in each of us that wants to lead. We all want to invest in something bigger than ourselves and more valuable than what we can do alone. Whether we have aspirations and calls to lead our family, community, non-profit, company, or local church, we all want to invest in something and someone. We all want to lead.

The issue that we're left with in all the noise and leadership talk is the gap between learning how to lead and actually becoming a good leader. No matter how strong of a call and anointing God has placed on us as leaders, we still have a duty and a call to go further and to sharpen our abilities. Jesus set the example in growth. While He was born perfect, He still grew in His abilities and calling. Luke 2:52 describes Jesus' growth this way: "And Jesus grew in wisdom and stature, and in favor with God and man."

How do we grow? We practice all the knowledge we gain from the resources we're given. Different people do this in different ways and grow in their own unique style. Much of what separates the great from the average, though, is how they react to the people, situations, and opportunities around them. How they are able to shift from just another voice in the crowd to the next great leader distinguishes them from the rest of the pack.

Leadership is about people. The great leaders are the ones who know how to treat people and move people to do something beyond what they can see for themselves. Those are the *next up* leaders. The ones who have the traits necessary to react to situations and value people. The leaders who are constantly improving themselves, their leadership capacity, and their organizations are the world's next great leaders. The ones who are able to serve people, love people, and grow in wisdom and stature and in favor with God are the leaders who get ahead. The leaders who possess the right principles for all their leadership knowledge to rest on are the ones who make an impact on the people around them.

> **WHETHER WE have aspirations and calls to lead our family, community, non-profit, company, or local church, we all want to invest in something and someone. We all want to lead.**

If you and I are going to become the leaders who apply the knowledge and information in a unique and purposeful way, we're going to have to shift the stereotypes that accompany our generation.

Too much rests on our generation getting down to business and leading the next great movement for us to stay the way we currently are. The information age we live in needs some people who are able to cut out the noise and apply the good stuff it brings.

A PRE-SHIFT

I'm not sure when it happened, but at some point in time, leadership development became an art in cloning the already existing leaders. So often, churches and organizations take potential leaders and begin to try and fit them into their mold of what a leader should look like. Instead of asking potential leaders to be themselves, develop some of their strengths, and adopt a few new ideas, many organizations have taught leaders how to walk, talk, act, think, and be exactly like the leaders they already have.

Becoming a *next up* leader doesn't mean you become just like the leader you're currently following. Becoming a *next up* leader and making the leadership shift means you become a better you who gleans and learns from the leaders in your life. Jesus never called His disciples to be exactly like each other—Jesus called them to follow Him.

You have something inside of you that God desperately wants to use. You have to make a shift in your mind before you can ever make a shift in your leadership. You have to go from thinking that you have to watch out of the window while others mow the grass to knowing that, with God's anointing and work through you, you can jump in and mow it yourself.

In order for you to change the world in our generation, you're going to have to shift from thinking, "I can't," to thinking, "I will." With that mindset, the gifts of God, and the guidance of the Holy Spirit, this generation can accomplish great things. We have the call. We have tools. We have to make these eight specific shifts and be ready to take the reins when the time comes.

#1

FROM *ENTITLEMENT* TO HONOR

The words *entitlement* and *honor* may not seem like they go together at first. After all, we don't necessarily think about the two being polar opposites. The truth is, though, that the millennial generation has forced the two to be mentioned in the same sentence . . . or at least in the same chapter!

If I were to poll one hundred people who claimed to understand what the millennial generation is and asked those people to name the top three problems with our generation, the majority of them would probably list a sense of entitlement as being one of the great problems. Whether completely true or not, young people today are often accused of believing they are entitled to certain rights and privileges in life.

I believe there is a lot of merit to the idea that our generation (those in their twenties and early thirties) is a generation that feels entitled to many things. It's not just physical things we feel entitled to either. Many in our generation feel entitled to happiness at any cost and entitled to respect and influence well before it's earned. For those of us looking to be the next great leaders who move our organizations, families, and churches forward, we have to understand that we're not entitled. We have to understand that, while we should certainly be respected to some degree, no one owes us great authority or influence.

WE AREN'T ENTITLED TO ANYTHING

If we feel entitled to something, we think we deserve it—that it should be ours just because we're us. The truth is, we don't deserve anything we're given. This is a concept we as Christians should understand. The only thing you and I really deserve is *nothing*. That's what we've earned.

Think back for a second to your childhood. If you were like me, you were blessed enough to have parents who loved and cared for you beyond what you could have ever earned. Really, I was blessed beyond belief because my mom had a hard time telling me no. Some would say I had her wrapped around my little kid finger. Mom had such a hard time telling me no she would always let me get a toy when we went to Wal-Mart. I remember searching the aisles over and over looking for that one toy I wanted to buy each time we went. At the end of the shopping trip, it was mine.

I was about eight years old the first time I can remember my mom telling me no on a Wal-Mart trip. This particular trip, I walked through the entrance, ran to the toy aisle, browsed for a while, grabbed my toy of choice, and met up with Mom a few aisles over. But this time when I took the toy over to Mom, she said, "No!"

I don't know if she was proving a point or if she had just had a parent epiphany that I couldn't always have my way, but she told me no. I couldn't believe it. I was her child! I deserved the toy! I was entitled to it! Many of us still have that mentality, even into our adult lives. We're convinced that because we are who we are, we deserve special treatment or something in return.

> **WE'VE DECIDED to sacrifice honor and love on the altar of proving ourselves and our theology to be right.**

Now, I don't think it's all on our own merit. Many times we're told we deserve something. Many of you had a mom like mine who, despite great intentions, was really good at spoiling her children. The belief that we're entitled grows over time. Each time we think, "I deserve that," or "Why don't I get that?" we let it grow a little more. Soon, entitlement is in our beliefs and it begins to drag us down and ruin our view of the world and of others.

THE DISCIPLINE OF HONOR

I remember flipping on the news right after the last presidential election and feeling stunned by the lack of honor the panelists and commentators showed toward both candidates. We've lost the idea of honor in our society. Society has quit teaching us how to honor others, how to honor our parents, and how to honor our leaders.

Do you remember the only one of the Ten Commandments that comes with a promise? Moses, after being called up on Mount Sinai, was issued commands for the people to live by. The one commandment God gave to Moses that was accompanied by a promise was the one that said, "*Honor* your father and your mother, so that you may *live long* in the land the Lord your God is giving you" (Exodus 20:12, emphasis mine). God told the people thousands of years ago that honoring those people God put in authority over them was important. In fact, God went as far as to say that the span of their lives hinged on it.

We've lost the concept of honoring our leaders, but we've also lost the concept of honoring our peers. Get on Twitter any day and you'll see people arguing back and forth, holding nothing back. Even in the church, we've lost the idea of honoring those around us. We've decided to sacrifice honor and love on the altar of proving ourselves and our theology to be right. In the meantime, we've become a church and society that has lost touch with honor. We've lost the idea that love and honor trump everything else.

DEFINING HONOR

Honor is one of those heroic sounding words. Read any good fairy tale and there's an honorable hero. Flip on most old movies and you'll find a man fighting for the honor of his lady. No matter what romance novel you read (so they tell me), the woman in the novel always wants an honorable man to come and rescue her from her situation or family. Honor has a long history and is a word that gets tossed around a lot, so how have we failed to display it? We've lost the meaning of real honor. We've lost the meaning of honoring others in our entitlement mindset and our selfish society. Honor means "a showing of usually merited respect."[1] Did you catch the key word in that definition? Go back and read it again. We leaders really need to pay attention to that

> HONORING GOD travels to everything we do, everything we say, and every decision we make.

word *usually*. You see, honor doesn't have to be merited. For believers in Christ, honor definitely doesn't have to be merited. The people around us and the leaders we serve with don't have to prove anything to us. The leaders we serve don't have to earn our honor. We should always give it regardless.

Honor and respect go hand in hand. We all desire to be respected. We all want to have people around us who appreciate us for who we are. We aren't entitled to respect, but we definitely want it. Honor isn't just something leaders should get, but also something we have to be extra assertive to give.

A PICTURE OF HONOR

The Bible is full of stories about honor. Beyond just telling us to honor our mother and father unconditionally, the Bible tells us to honor God, to honor our neighbors, and to honor our leaders. Honor can't be void of a loving heart and a forgiving mind. If we're going to make the shift from feeling like we're entitled to believing that we must honor others, we're going to have to realize that our goal is to give what others sometimes don't deserve.

Honor God

If we're going to become people who show honor, it begins with God. Making the shift with God specifically from entitlement to honor should be really simple. He's the Creator, the Sustainer, and the Provider—we are not. Honoring Him and loving Him should be our top priority. We have to honor God in every part of our lives, not just in the right context. I can't begin to count the number of young people and young leaders I speak with who are great at honoring God with their time on Sunday morning and are great at tweeting Bible verses, but fail to honor God with their work and their day-to-day lives. Honoring God is a 24/7 calling. Honoring God travels to everything we do, everything we say, and every decision we make.

In my life, one of the most challenging verses in all of Scripture is 1 Corinthians 10:31, which says, "So whether you eat or drink or whatever you do, do it all for the glory of God." Think about that for a second. If we obey this verse, loving and honoring God carries to every part of our lives. For young leaders, this is especially eye-opening. There may be times when it would be really easy for us to excel and get ahead, but it might not honor God. There are times when there may appear to be a fast track to a promotion or raise, but that fast track might not be honoring to God. For those of us who have a gifting for leading and influencing others, it can be really easy and seem really simple to step over people to get to where we think we need to go. In the heat of wanting to get to the top, we can often influence people to rally against someone else or against an idea. As heavy influencers, we can take advantage of someone's small mistake in order for us to get ahead. Again, that would be the easy thing, but not the God-honoring thing. To obey this verse, we have to use our gifts how God wants us to use them. See why that 1 Corinthians verse is so challenging? Honor God first.

Honor Others

The character of Uriah in 2 Samuel 11 is often overlooked in the Scripture. Uriah is rarely seen as heroic. He is usually seen as the guy who got the short end of the stick and was stabbed in the back by the people he trusted. If we take a look at the story, though, we see what kind of guy Uriah really was. He sets an unprecedented example in honoring the people around him. If you don't know the story, Uriah was out fighting with the rest of the Israelite army while David (the king) was back at home. One day, David is on his roof when he looks across the way and notices Uriah's wife, Bathsheba, bathing. David is immediately attracted to Bathsheba, so he sends for her and sleeps with her. David later gets word that he got Bathsheba pregnant. David, being the king, knows this is not a good move and goes into panic mode. Immediately, David sends for Uriah. Upon arrival, David tells him to go home to his wife. Uriah, not knowing about his wife's pregnancy, refuses to go home. What happens next shows what makes Uriah such an example of honor. In 2 Samuel 11:11 Uriah tells David, "The ark and Israel and Judah are staying in tents, and my commander Joab and my lord's men are camped in the open country. How could I go to my house to eat and drink and make love to my wife? As surely as you live, I will not do such a thing!"

Did you catch the significance of what Uriah did? Uriah not only honored his commander and leader, but he honored all those fighting with him by not going home. Uriah had too much respect for those he considered his peers to enjoy something he knew they couldn't. You and I sometimes have to give up what we feel entitled to in order to show honor to those around us.

I know you're thinking, "If you knew some of the people I know, you'd know that they don't deserve honor." Honor is shown even in the midst of what people don't deserve. Honor others anyway. Honor their time. Honor their lives. Honor their sacrifices.

Honor Your Leader

Growing up, my older brother, David, blazed the ministry and leadership trail before it was my time. David taught me a lot, but one of the most valuable things he taught me was how to show honor to the people who led me. Every now and then, I think back to where I've been and have to think that many of the blessings I've been given over my life are because I was taught how to show honor to the people God has placed over me.

One of the most obvious examples of honoring a leader is in the exchange between Saul and David in 1 Samuel 24. Saul was the king of Israel at the time, but he disobeyed God tremendously. David was the one God determined was going to be the next king of Israel. Saul, consumed with pride and jealousy, tried unceasingly to kill David before David got his chance to be king. David had done nothing wrong, but Saul was still determined to kill him. David could have easily justified speaking badly of Saul or even going ahead, rushing ahead of God, and killing Saul on the spot. Instead though, David, having Saul cornered and in a vulnerable position, decided not to rise up against Saul. In fact, David refused to even say anything bad about his leader and in 1 Samuel 24:6 says, "The Lord forbid that I should do such a thing to my master, the Lord's anointed, or lay my hand on him; for he is the anointed of the Lord." Wow! That's honor. Saul did nothing to deserve it. God had placed Saul in his high position, and David recognized it. Even though David had every right to feel entitled to kill Saul since God had anointed David and told him his enemies would be delivered into his hands, he left entitlement behind to show honor to his leader.

Just like David, we have to be people who honor our leaders. We have to serve our leaders, not because our leaders always deserve honor or serving, but because it allows us the freedom to resist entitlement. Don't use honor as a manipulative tactic either. When you honor the person who leads you or who signs your check or who has the power to hire and fire you, don't do it to manipulate them. David didn't honor Saul in hopes of getting a fatter calf out of the deal. We honor our leaders out of recognition for who they are and appreciation for the duty they have. The second you and I begin to show honor to our leader because we want something in return is the second our honor turns back into entitlement.

MAKING THE SHIFT

How do we go from being people who feel entitled to people who are great at showing others honor? In order to be the next up to take the leadership reins, we're going to have to make the shift. In my experience, the people around us know when we're leading from a place of selfishness and false humility. When they see our entitled mindset, they'll be quick to cut us off and begin to do just enough to get by.

Know Your Leader

As we learn to honor God, we have to begin making the shift in honoring our leader. We have to understand the people who do their best to lead us and the organization that we love and work for are only human. You see, many times we fail to respect people and honor people because we forget they're flawed human beings just like us. If we expect others to offer us grace, we must be willing to do the same, even if they're in leadership above us. Regardless of our relationships with our leaders, they will disappoint us. At times, they may fail to show us the honor that we feel we have earned. We'll be disappointed in our leaders from time to time for making the decision they made or for treating someone else in a way we didn't see fit. We have to honor them anyway.

Understand that your leaders aren't perfect and understand that your job as a follower is to support them. The truth is, those leaders at high levels (the level you may be striving toward) bear heavy loads. Honor your leaders and support them. In Exodus 17, we get a great picture of some followers supporting their leader. Moses commanded the people to go fight the Amalekites (yeah, I'm not sure how to say it either) while he held up his staff to God so they could win the fight. During the fight, Moses' arms started to get tired. Every time Moses' hands began to fall, the Amalekites excelled in the battle. So what did Aaron and Hur (the people with Moses at the time) do? They supported Moses' arms so that he could hold his hands up. That's a great picture of what supporting your leader should look like.

Know Yourself

If we're going to make the shift from entitlement to honor, we're going to have to know our leader, but also know ourselves. Do you understand who you are? You are something only because of what Christ did for you. In fact, according to Romans 5:8, you were nothing but a sinner when the Savior of the world chose to honor you and die for your sin. Who are we, not to honor those around us?

SHIFT SHAPERS

To make the shift from entitlement to honor, you have to believe . . .

1. You are not entitled to rewards, only indebted to Christ.
2. Honoring God comes before honoring others.
3. Honor continues even when others don't deserve it.

Honor God by honoring others. #NextUpBook

#2

FROM *UNRELIABLE* TO CONSISTENT

There are no two words that can make or break a person's reputation faster than the words *unreliable* and *consistent*. Each of those words brings up certain mental images when we hear them. *Unreliable* and *consistent* create powerful ideas because they are directly associated with our character. They describe not just what we act like but who we are as people and as leaders.

My first car was a 1997 Pontiac Grand Am. It had about 100,000 miles on it from a previous owner when I got it. Didn't matter—it was all new to me. It doesn't seem like much of a car now, but as a newly licensed sixteen-year-old driver, that car meant so much to me. I had, for what felt like the first time in my life, *freedom*. That car represented more than just a means of transportation to me, it represented my ability to have fun, make friends, make memories, and be me.

My Pontiac Grand Am was a good car. It got me from place to place in one piece—for a year or so. The first time it let me down was on a first date with a girl I had been chasing after for months. She finally agreed to go out with me (I finally had the guts to ask) and give me a shot. I spent hours getting that car to look the best it could. We went out that night for dinner and a movie. At the time, I was sure I was going to marry her. I may have only been seventeen, but I just knew I was about to win over the woman of my dreams.

After the movie that night, we decided to hit up a drive-through for a milkshake before I took her home. About three minutes into our wait at the drive-through line, I started seeing smoke billow out from under the hood. "Maybe she won't notice. Just pretend like it isn't there," I told myself. So I stayed cool, thinking that when we started moving, the problem would resolve itself. Well, we didn't start moving again. The car smoked more and more as we sat in line. Eventually, I pulled my red Grand Am over into a parking spot and waited for my dad to come and get us. I was humiliated. The date went from being a successful night to a failure with a girl who probably never cared to see me again.

Over the next few months, the car was in and out of the shop several times. It often ran hot when it idled and the gas gauge became very inaccurate. The car became too unreliable. It was no longer a symbol of my freedom and future; it became a symbol of inconsistency and unreliability.

Our value as leaders hinges greatly on our ability to be consistent in our lives and leadership. It's vitally important that we prove to ourselves, the people who lead us, and the people we lead that we are consistent people and leaders. We're valuable as pictures of consistency; when we become unreliable, though, we lose much of our value to the people we lead and the organizations we serve.

DEFINING UNRELIABLE

As a child, I was blessed with people I could always depend on. One of those people who always had my back was my dad. My dad is the model of consistency. For as long as I can remember, my dad has worn the same hairstyle, had the same wardrobe, and maintained the same level of integrity. He's always been reliable to me. Growing up, he was always there for me. Countless times as an adult, I have been able to rely on Dad as well. Just a few weeks ago, I called him about a problem with our house. You see, we're recent home buyers, and I have little to no construction or household-repair knowledge. Dad picked up the phone and, as he always does, walked me through the problem. At the end of that phone call, Dad told me the same thing he says every time I talk to him: "Jonathan, if you need me, you know where to find me."

I want to be like my dad in his reliability and integrity. In fact, I'm sure there's not a person reading this right now who wants to be considered unreliable. Having an unreliable reputation is one of those things we gain over time but can hardly ever shake once we claim it. We usually begin relationships with people, no matter the context, with a positive reputation in their minds. For the most part, people are forgiving when we show some level of unreliability to them. Most people will overlook our lack of preparation or scheduling for a little while. Most people understand that things come up and that everyone tends to overpromise at times. Eventually, though, people will begin to see us as

PREPARATION
prevents unreliability.

unreliable if we continue to display those unreliable characteristics. It takes years of consistency, proving ourselves, and building trust to change our reputation ... if we're ever able to change it.

In the end, whether we mean to or not, when we become unreliable people, we say something to people we're close to and the people we let down. Unreliability really says, "I don't care." Think about it, we usually make time for the things we care most about. When we have to drop the ball on something or let go of something, it's usually the thing we care less about. When we become unreliable, we show we don't care. Unreliability also displays a lack of preparation. Preparation prevents unreliability. When you and I properly prepare for what we know is coming by making time and thinking ahead, we avoid becoming unreliable.

DEFINING CONSISTENT

Being disciplined enough to do the same thing with regularity is consistency. What does that mean for us as young leaders? It means that consistency proves our potential. Unlike my old Grand Am, we have to be young people who prove that we're worth an investment. Consistency goes a long way in proving that we do have the potential to lead big in the future.

Consistency Means Survival

A few years ago, my wife and I decided that we wanted to grow our own vegetables. We lived in the country at the time and had plenty of room to plant a few fresh veggies. As we thought about and talked through the idea, we could just taste the perfectly cultivated squash, zucchini, tomatoes, and peppers. We were going to kick it old school and produce our own food. We knew it was going to be a great way to enjoy some time outdoors, spend some time together, and save a few dollars along the way.

The day after Melissa and I talked about starting a garden, we went to the store and bought some plants and seeds. We must have been the ideal garden store customers. We had little knowledge about growing anything, so we bought just about anything the guy helping us suggested. From fertilizers to equipment to hoses, we went home with the perfect setup to begin our own garden. We got home, began to churn up some of the ground as best we knew how, and started planting our veggies. We were so excited about those little green plants that we spent the first week paying close attention to them, watering them, giving them food, and pulling anything that looked like a possible weed.

A couple of weeks into gardening, we were a little less excited about growing our own vegetables. We went out and checked on the garden and weeded it every few days. As the summer went on, it became fewer and further between. Needless to say, we weren't very successful in our gardening experiment. At the end of the summer, I remember looking at Melissa one day as we were in the backyard and saying, "Gosh, could you imagine being a farmer and having to do this to survive?" Consistency is needed for survival.

Consistency is one of the most important shifts that great young leaders make. When we become people who are willing to keep working and stay consistent even when it's not easy, convenient, or going the way we want, we start to be people who know how to move forward regardless of the problems that may come our way. In leadership and life, it's invaluable that we know how to move on from hurts and pain and failure. People who know how to maintain consistency in the heart of disruption and disaster are irreplaceable. Developing consistency will go a long way in becoming a *next up* leader.

The Consistency Test

It doesn't take a great leader or a great young person to do something *occasionally*. For years, I couldn't bring myself to exercise consistently. Sure, I could go for a jog or go play basketball or work out with someone on occasion. Sure, I would always say in my head that it wasn't going to be a one-time thing, but it always was. It doesn't take a great leader to do something once. It only takes someone with a moment of motivation—it doesn't require a strong conviction. Consistency requires conviction. In order for us to do something consistently, we have to have a conviction that the end result is worth it. That's why consistency is such an important shift for our leaders to see in our lives: it shows our commitment to the organization, non-profit, or church we help lead.

CONSISTENCY requires conviction.

Young people especially often lack this conviction to do something consistently. We as a generation are quickly motivated by a need and are great at rallying to meet those needs. We aren't, however, great at consistency. That's why we can rally thousands of people to lead a Twitter protest or lend aid after a natural disaster, but we fail to help reduce homelessness in our communities. Being a catalyst for lasting cultural changes requires long-term action and commitment on our part. It requires our consistent thought and effort. Many of us lack the conviction to do something consistently. We often choose instead to do things as quickly as possible. What ends up happening is that we run from need to need, cause to cause, leadership role to leadership role, and fail to truly invest. If we're going to be the generation that takes the leadership hand-off and moves our organizations into the next few decades, we're going to have to find the conviction of consistency.

Consistency is the thing that will separate the next generation of great leaders from the rest of the pack. Consistency to try, consistency to show up, consistency to do the right thing, and consistency to work hard will be the very things that allow certain young leaders to make it.

One of the reasons I love Major League Baseball is because of the length of their season. Some hate baseball for the same reason, but I think it's what really separates it from other sports. During a 162-game MLB season, we get to see the teams that are consistently the best. Over the course of 162 games, teams and players will go through streaks of greatness and streaks of lackluster play. The players and teams who consistently improve and consistently play well are the ones who end up in the playoffs at the end of the year. There's no doubt at the end of the season who has the best team. The best teams at the end of the season are the ones who played with consistent conviction. Are you the kind of leader who will rise above the rest because of your consistency?

CONSISTENCY MODEL

No one models consistency like our Creator Himself. God is the picture of consistency. Throughout the course of history, God has not changed. God was the same the day He created the world as He is today. God was the same when He made a covenant with Abraham as He is today. God was the same when He sent Jesus as He is today. God's character is consistent. God never changes. That's one of the things that makes God so unique and great. We can trust that what God has done in the past, what God has promised in the past, and what God has said in the past reflects who He is today. God has always loved His people as much as He loves you and me right now. Nothing has ever changed in God's love meter.

He has never once had a day where He decided to step back and not have control of the world and our lives. God is the model of consistency. Revelation 22:13 says, "I am the Alpha and the Omega, the First and the Last, the Beginning and the End." God always has been and always will be.

A CONSISTENT LIFE

Leading consistently begins with living consistently. Now, I'm not saying there's no room for spur-of-the-moment camping trips or impromptu, late-night get-togethers with friends. Things like this help refresh us. What I mean is that our day-to-day lives should have some level of consistency in them. I know this can be hard for young people. For some, that's because what they do on a daily basis is out of their control. For others, living consistently is hard because you are truly still trying to figure out who you want to be as a self-supporting adult. We still have to find a way to make the shift to consistency in our daily lives.

You *are* what you consistently *do*. Who we really are is reflected in our hearts. As we go about our days and move from place to place, talk with different people, and react to different situations, our true character is on display. Life is going to throw some curveballs—consistency in how we handle life, though, proves who we really are.

> **LEADING CONSISTENTLY begins with living consistently.**

Our leadership reflects our lives. We'd all like to think we can separate our personal life from our leadership life, but it's just not possible. Who you are and what you consistently do is going to be reflected in the way you lead. If you hold to one set of morals in your everyday life, don't expect to be able to flip a switch when you get to work. If you treat people one way when you're away from the office or the people you lead, don't expect to be able to treat people differently when you're at the office and around those people.

Do you remember the parable in Matthew 18 about the unmerciful servant? In that chapter, Peter asked Jesus a question about forgiving other people. The parable teaches forgiveness, but also gives us an idea of what God thinks about inconsistencies. Jesus responded with a parable about a king who forgave one of his servants for owing him ten thousand bags of gold. The same servant later went out and found one of his fellow servants who owed him one hundred silver coins. The Bible says the first servant began to choke the man who owed him, demanding he pay back his debt. The servant with the debt began to plead with the man to be patient while he scraped up the money to pay him back. But the servant refused to forgive the debt or allow the other servant to wait to get the money. Not long after that, another servant who saw the encounter between the two servants went to the master and told him what the servant had done. Upon hearing the news, the king had the first servant put in jail until he could pay the debt he had owed.

The master saw the inconsistencies in the first servant's life and reacted in anger. You and I can't lead lives of inconsistency and expect to lead people to a place of greatness. We have to shift to being consistent in how we live and how we lead.

Leading Consistently

When I first began writing this book, I have to admit that I was overwhelmed. In the spirit of confession, I'm more of a bullet point guy than a paragraph and chapter person. The thought of writing a book kept me up at night. I knew, though, that God was calling me to write about these eight shifts. So I agreed to begin the process of writing what you're now reading. When I began to type out the first chapter, I was thinking, "There's no way I have the patience to type all this out. It will take months!" I was right, it did take months to put it together. However, a couple of weeks into the writing process, I remembered the old Creighton Abrams quote that says, "When eating an elephant, take one bite at a time." This meant that in order to write a chapter, I had to write words. In order to write a book, I had to write chapters. So I decided that instead of being overwhelmed with a lot of words, I was going to eat the elephant little by little. Consistently eating the elephant is much easier than trying to fit the entire thing in our mouth at one time.

Leadership often has those "eat an elephant" moments. There are times when, as young leaders, we'll look around and have no idea where to start. When staff are having problems, when things seem to be stalled, when what used to work doesn't anymore and needs to be changed, and when donations aren't coming in, the elephant can be huge. We have to lead consistently or we'll be eaten by the elephant. That's why it's so important for each of us to develop consistency in our lives now and shift from being unreliable to consistent. If we make the adjustments now, we'll be much more capable when the elephant arrives later.

MAKING THE SHIFT

How do we make the shift from unreliable to consistent? It certainly doesn't happen overnight. Even in making a shift in our leadership makeup, we're going to have to know what it's like to eat an elephant one bite at a time.

Recognize the Benefits

Just like living and leading consistently begins with a conviction, so does making the shift to consistency. If you're going to make the necessary shift (and it is a necessary one), you're going to first have to recognize the benefits of making it. Only upon knowing the benefit of something will we begin to put it into practice.

Consistency is a fast way to build influence. Don't take that statement as an avenue for manipulation or getting a leg up on the people around you, but leadership requires influence. Young leaders can't rely as heavily on past experiences and age-old relationships the same way older leaders can. Where you and I lack as young leaders, we can gain some ground by being people of consistency. I wanted to run my Grand Am off a cliff because it was so inconsistent and unreliable. Just like that, unreliable people get dismissed. We want to be around people and want to be led by people who display consistency.

> ONLY UPON knowing the benefit of something will we begin to put it into practice.

Plan Ahead

If you want to make the shift from unreliable to consistent, plan ahead. Planning is something that many in our generation aren't very good at doing. We have so many ways to make lists, be productive, and keep calendars, yet many of us fail to plan ahead. We often fail to plan out our week or day. Begin organizing for consistency now. Your calendar may not be full right now, you may have room for margin, but you still need to plan as if you're top-of-the-leadership-ladder busy. Creating that habit now and knowing how to manage your time will go a long way later when time becomes a valuable asset and consistency becomes seemingly impossible. Consistency in life and in leadership means we plan ahead for it.

Be Realistic

I can't count the number of times in my life that I've disappointed myself because I set an unrealistic goal or made an impossible promise. After the fact, I'll look back and notice that I have seemed unreliable, but it's really because I was unrealistic in the first place. No matter our age, we can only do so much. The temptation for young people, especially leaders, is to accept every invitation and agree to do everything in order to prove ourselves quickly. If you're not careful, you're going to end up looking unreliable instead of leadership ready. Operate within your schedule and your gifting.

SHIFT SHAPERS

To make the shift from unreliable to consistent, you have to believe . . .

1. What you do consistently proves who you really are.
2. Consistency is a secret weapon to being next up.

You are what you do consistently. Anyone can do something once—champions are the ones who repeat it. #NextUpBook

#3

FROM *DISSENSION* TO COOPERATION

I can't think of very many leadership conferences I've attended or leadership books I've read that talked about dissension and cooperation as being extremely pertinent to leadership and to each other. The truth is, though, these two words are often the very things that cause teams to work well together and move a vision forward or cause teams to unravel from the inside out.

If you and I are serious about being *next up* kind of leaders, we're going to have to make a shift in our thinking. We're going to have to turn our focus toward being a concentrated, cooperative member of the teams we work and serve on. This is about being a catalyst for cooperation.

DIVISION IS EASIER

Dissension divides teams and vision. It's something we're all guilty of causing—at least occasionally. Very early in life, all humans learn that it's important to fight for yourself. No one has ever had to teach a newborn baby to cry when they're hungry. No one has ever had to train a child to pitch a temper tantrum when they don't get their way. No parent has ever trained their teenager to yell at them when they aren't allowed to stay out late with friends. You and I are born in a fallen state. You and I know how to fight for ourselves. We know how to be selfish. For many of us, we learn over time to bridle some of our selfishness. Most people learn at some point in their lives that it's wise to give back and invest in other people. Still, though, we live with a desire to have things our way, to get what we want, and to go to great lengths to get it.

Dissension is a product of that selfishness that all of us are born with. Dissension is the thing that creeps its way through our attempts to manipulate others and have our way in a situation. Dissension finds its way into our lives and leadership by making us fight for our own agenda. Dissension says things like, "If I don't look out for myself, no one will." Dissension finds its way into our hearts and minds when we think, "It doesn't matter what they think; it's time I get my way." Dissension is even present when we think, "My way will be better in the long run." You see, dissension is a tricky animal. Dissension, when allowed to stay around, can cause great damage to our relationships and careers.

An attitude of dissension has led to destroyed marriages, collapsed empires, and ruined societies. Dissension is no joke. Each of us has a tendency to cause it. Each of us is to blame when it happens. Dissension is the thing we sow when we argue with someone just because we can. Or better yet, it's an attitude that looks to argue and disagree before trying to comply. It often comes from a place of feeling like we know best or not wanting to admit someone else does. Many times, we sow dissension into our culture and surroundings unknowingly. Sometimes, dissension is something we have little control over. There are certain issues we sometimes have to make an argument for that may sow seeds of dissension.

On the other hand, sometimes we bring dissension into our surroundings willingly and knowingly. It's those times we intentionally cause dissension that will keep us from being a *next up* kind of leader. It's those times we say a little something to take a shot at someone who's been getting on our nerves or those times when we go against the people in the room just to prove a point that we have to shift away from. Dissension kills momentum in our lives and in our places of leadership. It slows us down and causes us to lose focus on the real task at hand. Dissension, when we're the source of it, can stunt our leadership growth and stop us from becoming the leader we have the potential to be.

DEFINING COOPERATION

I ran my first road race about a year ago. In fact, up until about three years ago, I never worked out regularly or ran for anything except to a good buffet line. So, you can imagine my nervousness about committing to run a race of any length. When a friend of mine first asked me about it, I was already running around my neighborhood on occasion. I'd run a couple of miles a few times a week as a way of burning some calories and getting my heart rate up. Committing to run a road race, though, was an entirely different thing!

About a month before the race, I decided I would try to run a 12k on my own, as that's how long the road race was. About four miles into the seven and a half miles that a 12k consists of, I found myself about to fall out into traffic from exhaustion. I huffed and puffed my way home that day, then texted my friend and said something like, "Seriously getting worried about this thing. They may have to call an ambulance for me about five miles in!" Even with the apprehension, I kept my commitment and continued to train for the 12k. We finally came to the week of the race, and I still hadn't run over five miles.

Much to my disappointment, race day finally came (my hope of Jesus coming back the night before didn't happen). So I woke up to an early alarm clock. I got up, got dressed, stretched, and headed out for the race. The gun fired, my friend and I took off, and I remember thinking, "Okay, Jonathan, go slow the whole way and you may make it." About four miles into the race was the first time I felt even faintly out of breath. By mile seven, I was getting tired but knew I had enough in the tank to finish it. During the final stretch of the race, one of the guys I had been running beside challenged me to a sprint to the finish line. I sprinted as hard as I could go. As I crossed the line, I felt like I still had another mile or two in me.

You see, the reason running long distances is so much easier when we're in a race is because we are running with other people. Life and leadership are like that. When you and I have people around us who are doing the same things we're doing, working toward the same goals we're working toward, and making the same sacrifices we're making, what we're doing becomes so much easier. That's why cooperation is not only important to our leadership future, but important to our everyday lives. We have to have people around us we can cooperate with and confide in.

Cooperation doesn't happen for the benefit of one person or to put one person on a pedestal and have them run the show. Cooperation is not about pleasing other people and rolling over when tough conversations have to happen. Cooperation isn't spineless floundering when the people around you or over you need to be told something tough. Cooperation is thinking of others, hearing others, and finding middle ground. Cooperation is realizing where many can benefit from many different voices. Cooperation is knowing that many can grow by many getting to participate. Cooperation is a necessary shift.

I have to admit, cooperation isn't easy. For me, as a young leader, and one with passion and excitement for what I do, cooperation can be a difficult concept to understand and practice. For us as a generation, cooperation is tough because, quite frankly, we haven't had to do it a lot. Many of us grew up being able to have it our way. Cooperation is one of those life and leadership principles that becomes easier once we experience it.

COOPERATION BEGINS HERE

Cooperation, like so many great life and leadership principles, begins with how we see and value others. The reality is, if we see others as less valuable and as nothing more than tools to get our way, we aren't going to get cooperation right. We have to

> **PEOPLE ARE God's priority, so people are a leader's priority.**

see people the way their Creator sees them. People are not a project for us. People are valuable to God and they have to be valuable to us. As leaders, people have to be our top priority.

There have been numerous times when I have been sitting at my desk just starting to prepare a teaching or do some writing, and am paged about someone needing a person to talk to. My immediate thought always goes toward dissension and thinking that what I'm about to do is more important. Then I remember and remind myself that people are my priority. People are God's priority, so people are a leader's priority. The most well-known verse in the Bible reminds us just how much God values people and what great lengths He's willing to go to in order to love people. John 3:16 says, "For *God so loved the world* that he gave his one and only Son, that whoever believes in him shall not perish but have eternal life" (emphasis mine). God values you, He values me, He values the people who lead you and the people you will lead.

God values cooperation and unity. One of the greatest illustrations of cooperation at work is the local church working together. I love the way Paul paints the picture in 1 Corinthians 12:12 when he says, "Just as a body, though one, has many parts, but all its many parts form one body, so it is with Christ." If we fully understand what Paul is saying, we understand that, in order to be one, we have to cooperate with each other. It's no mistake that God would want His church to operate in cooperation with each other. God knows that, when working together, we can do so much more than many of us working alone could ever complete. God's plan to work together must become our practice.

COOPERATION COUNTS

Cooperating with others has so many benefits for them and for us. Once we understand the full magnitude of working alongside other people and listening to different opinions and ideas, we begin to realize how important cooperating with those around us can be.

Cooperation is a good thing for each of us because it takes the pressure off. If we as young leaders can grasp the concept of unity and cooperation, we'll be free later from the stress of leading on an island. Working with churches in small towns across the country, I've heard so many times about how lonely some church leaders feel. It's not just that those leaders don't have anyone close to them to be honest with, it's that they feel lonely in finding vision, making decisions, and moving forward. Leadership can be a lonely venture, but when we cooperate, it becomes a little easier. No longer do we have to make a decision and hope that people will buy in to it; when we're cooperating with other people and hearing their opinions, we know they will. When we cooperate, no longer do we have to do all of the work because it was our idea; we'll have other people help us with some of the heavy lifting because they had a hand in forming the idea.

Even now, before you and I go to the next place in leadership, we have to understand that cooperation is better than competition. I know the temptation to try and compete with the people around us. When there seems to be a job opening in a higher position or when evaluations come up, it can be easy to switch on our competitive box and compete with the people we work with. It's really tempting to get into a meeting or into a discussion and compete for our idea or thought to be chosen as the one to go with. Let cooperation win out. Make cooperating with your peers and coworkers what you're known for.

MAKING THE SHIFT

Making the shift from dissension to cooperation is one of the things you and I could look back on years from now and mention as one of the most pivotal things we did in our leadership career. Going from a person who is naturally bent to sow seeds of dissension to a person who makes cooperating a habit is important if we're going to be looked at as a *next up* leader. Speaking with senior leaders in different organizations, I've come to realize that cooperation is one of the things they first look for when making hires and promotions. They realize the importance of being able to work together as a team. Making the shift from dissension to cooperation will require each of us to put our pride in our pocket and step up to the table with an eye on accomplishing great things for the people and organizations we serve.

Adopt the Humility Habit

Leading requires humility. If we don't show humility as leaders, leadership will eventually humble us on its own. Cooperation requires that same humility. Making the shift from dissension to cooperation will mean we won't always get our way and our ideas won't always be chosen. A humility habit continues to operate in cooperation with those around it, even when it doesn't get its way. A lot of the young people and professionals I talk to have yet to put away their childish selfishness. A lot of us have never lost the idea that we want what we want and we want it now. One of the verses I remind myself of most often when it comes to my attempt at cooperation is 1 Corinthians 13:11, "When I was a child, I talked like a child, I thought like a child, I reasoned like a child. When I became a man, I put the ways of childhood behind me." We have to be young leaders who put childhood behind us and move on to what's next. Live and lead from humility, not childish selfishness.

Value Diversity

The church I currently serve is a multiethnic church. We have a wide range of ages, races, and backgrounds. I remember the first Sunday I ever attended a service at Cornerstone Church. My wife and I walked in and sat down well before the service began. We didn't pay much attention to the people coming in after us. As we stood for the first song, though, we looked around and I quietly whispered, "This is what heaven is going to be like. They aren't all like us." I remember the grin that my wife had on her face as the service continued. Now, I hear stories like that all the time. I hear how much people love that not everyone who comes through our doors is like them. Why? Cornerstone values diversity. We plan diversity into everything we do, display, and say.

If we're going to make the shift from dissension to cooperation, we're going to have to value diversity. We'll have to value diversity in the people around us, what they look like and where they come from, but also in their thoughts and opinions. It goes back to valuing other people. When we value other people the way God values them, we value diversity and are willing to listen to other people . . . even if they're not like us.

The shift from being someone bent toward dissension to becoming someone who cooperates with the people around them won't feel natural at first. Make the shift anyway. For yourself, your family, your future, and for the organization you love—make the choice to cooperate.

SHIFT SHAPERS

To make the shift from dissension to cooperation, you have to believe . . .

1. Others are valuable to me because they are valuable to God.
2. Cooperation is important to others, but I also benefit from making it a habit.
3. Cooperation with others allows me to see what I can't see by myself and get ideas I can't think of myself.

Disagreement doesn't have to mean dissension. Work together. #NextUpBook

#4

FROM *CONFORMITY* TO INTEGRITY

If you've ever put up a basketball hoop or built a deck around your house, you understand how concrete conforms to the exact shape and size of the hole it is poured into. Over time, the concrete hardens into a permanent fixture inside the hole. Concrete hardens because it undergoes a chemical reaction as the air sets in it and dries it out. The very integrity and makeup of the wet concrete changes over time and becomes whatever its surroundings dictate.

Many in our generation are like that wet concrete. We're great at adapting to the people, places, and pressures around us. Integrity, though, takes work. Integrity is one of those character traits we all desire to have, but the pressures around us and the desire to get ahead often overtakes it. If you and I are going to be *next up* kind of leaders, we're going to have to adjust how we get ahead and how we react to what's around us.

WHY WE CONFORM

"I love Jimi Hendrix." That was one of the things I remember repeating in high school to a certain group of friends that I wanted to fit in with. Every day, this group of friends would sit around at lunch and after school with their guitars, strumming different tunes. I had no guitar (or guitar talent), but I wanted to be like those who did. They loved listening to Jimi Hendrix and humming his songs as they did their homework after school. I decided one day that if I was going to hang out with these guys, I had to like Jimi Hendrix. So, I went after school one day to the store and picked up one of his CDs. I put it on in my car and began to listen. I wouldn't have admitted it at the time, but I hated listening to Jimi Hendrix. Don't get me wrong, he was a great guitar player, but listening to his songs just didn't do it for me. It wasn't me. I was more Creed and Newsboys—not Jimi Hendrix.

> ## CONFORMITY IS when we do something because everyone else seems to do it.

I didn't realize it then, but what I was doing while I pretended to like Jimi Hendrix was conforming to the people around me. I was trying to lie to myself and those around me in order to get where I wanted to go, which was the guitar players' circle at school. That's the way conformity works. Usually, we agree to conform because we anticipate a given result on the other end of conforming. I expected to be able to hang out with the guitar players by conforming to what they liked. It isn't that much different for a young leader. We conform in order to get what we want. It's easy for us to give a little on excellence when everyone around us is doing the same. As young people, it's easy for us to cheat the time card in order to get home a little early. As young leaders, it's easy for us to talk about the boss behind their back in order to get a leg up on a relationship with someone else.

Conformity is when we do something because everyone else seems to do it. It's when we have an idea we think could be great but decide to do what others have always done instead. Conformity is meeting a *usual* or a standard. As leaders, we have to come to the place where we realize we aren't "standard." Now, don't get me wrong; we can't say we're better than anyone else, but we have to set a high standard for ourselves. We have to be willing to be constantly seeking to go above the requirement. That's what excellence is. That's what leadership is. As young leaders, especially young Christian leaders, we can't conform to an unwritten standard or give in to an outside pressure.

When Conformity Is Commendable

Before moving on, I have to say conforming *can* be a good thing. Conformity can be an appropriate action. Think back to the concrete I mentioned earlier. If concrete never conformed to what it was poured into, there would be millions and millions of buildings and structures all across the world that would be lying on the ground. The conformity of concrete is a good thing. Conformity can be a good thing for us too.

One of the early lessons I learned as a young pastor was the importance of being willing to conform. I've never forgotten the conversation my lead pastor had with me about three weeks into working at a church I served in. I was a confident young leader, well ahead of the curve. I was in a new situation in a new city and was doing everything I could to prove myself. The first few weeks I was there, I knew I was doing a good job. One Sunday, right before the day began, my pastor took me to the side and said, "Jonathan, I know you like to dress that way, but these people here aren't going to respect you like that. They're in a whole other ballpark and culture than what you're dressing for." I left that conversation wondering what exactly I had on that he didn't like. Several days later, I came to the realization it wasn't just about how I was dressed, but it was about their culture. You see, they loved their culture and they were never going to give respect to someone unwilling to be a part of it.

Conforming in order to relate to the people around us is a good and necessary thing. Conforming in order to earn the respect of people is commendable as long as we don't go against our moral standards. As young and second-chair leaders, we also have to conform to the vision of our senior leaders. It's absolutely essential for us to wrap our minds around the vision they have for our organization. If we're hoping to be the one who takes the leadership handoff, we're going to have to conform to our organization's systems and procedures.

When Conformity Isn't Commendable

Conformity isn't always a good thing. One of my favorite characters in the entire Bible is Daniel. He was a *next up* kind of leader. The people around Daniel recognized his potential from the time he was young. In fact, so much so that they named him to become part of the king's service. Daniel was the "who's who" of his day. Daniel was happy to have someone invest in him, but he wasn't willing to conform to what they had for him to eat. The menu the king was going to serve to his young men wasn't in accordance with Jewish law. Daniel refused to conform to his surroundings and asked the chief official for permission to eat vegetables instead. In fact, Daniel issued a little challenge to the chief official and asked that he and some of the ones selected along with him could eat only vegetables and water while the rest of the men ate what the king had selected for them. At the end of the challenge, Daniel and the guys who ate vegetables were healthier and better nourished. In the end, all the men were given the food Daniel asked to eat. Why was Daniel able to change what all the people around him were eating? Daniel was unwilling to conform to what he believed was wrong. When given the opportunity, Daniel refused to defile himself and take a hit to his integrity by doing something he felt strongly about not doing.

What Daniel did is a difficult test for young leaders. It's really easy for us to conform to what's around us in order to get what seems like an upper hand—but that's not commendable. As young people, it's really easy for us to conform to what's around us in order to build relationship and find friendship—that's not commendable. As a generation, we've become really good at conforming to what seems like *normal*. We've become too good at putting our beliefs and what we know is right aside in order to gain something in the short term. We have to make a shift. We have to move from conformity to integrity.

A PICTURE OF INTEGRITY

When it's all said and done, integrity comes down to moral values. Our integrity is really our ability to stick to what we believe—no matter the consequences. What made Daniel so strong as a young leader was his intense desire to avoid crossing what he believed was a moral line. You and I have to have that same kind of integrity. Not that we avoid eating certain foods (although that may be what it means to you), but that we avoid crossing the line on the moral values we have set in place in our lives. Doing what they know they shouldn't is really where most young people get integrity wrong. It usually begins with a temptation to do something that would show a slight lapse in integrity. Once we give in to the integrity lapse, it becomes much easier for us to do it time and time again. Before we know it, we've crossed the integrity line so many times that we've almost forgotten where it is. The people around you and the people leading you know where that line is. If you and I are going to take the leadership handoff, we're going to have to maintain the integrity line as well. Giving in once is too much.

Daniel refused to give in, even once. In Daniel 6, he finds himself in the position that many of us do today. Daniel is the up-and-coming leader. Daniel is in a position where he's being groomed to take a step up in his leadership position. Daniel really didn't need anything to go wrong. If he could have just continued on the track he was on, he would have inherited the entire kingdom. When Daniel got word, however, that a decree had been announced and no one could worship or pray to a god other than the king for thirty days, he didn't conform. In fact, Daniel 6 says explicitly that Daniel went upstairs, opened the window, and prayed three times a day to God and praised Him for all that He had done. Of course, Daniel got caught. The king, having made the decree, had to punish him. The king ordered that Daniel be thrown in the lions' den. Overnight, Daniel wasn't harmed by the lions. In fact, the next morning the king hurried to the den and was shocked when he called Daniel's name and got a response. Daniel was unwilling to budge on his

> **WE'VE BECOME too good at putting our beliefs and what we know is right aside in order to gain something in the short term.**

integrity and determination to do what was right.

Holding on to integrity will not necessarily shut the lions' mouths, but it will have its rewards. Daniel 6:28 goes on to say, "So Daniel prospered during the reign of Darius and the reign of Cyrus the Persian." God blessed Daniel's determination to maintain his integrity and not give in to worshiping an idol. Unfortunately, you and I often sacrifice God's prosperity on the altar of worshiping someone or something and giving our integrity away. That's what happens when we begin to chase after the approval of someone else above the approval of our Creator. In order to maintain a high level of integrity, we have to keep focused on our God. We have to lead ourselves well. We have to lead ourselves to resist conforming to what's not acceptable around us.

INTEGRITY TODAY

The king hasn't recently declared we shouldn't worship anyone but him. Lions' dens aren't commonplace in most of today's cities. Holding fast to our integrity won't look like it did for Daniel. For us leading and living today, holding on to integrity may mean that we refuse to dishonor our leader or that we refuse to give less than our full effort.

Integrity Means Admitting Our Shortcomings

"Leaders don't make mistakes." At least that's what I was led to believe for a long time. If leaders did make mistakes, they were savvy enough and smart enough to cover them up and make them look like odd but strategic moves. If you hold to that idea, I'm going to let you in on a secret . . . it's a lie. Leaders do make mistakes. There's never been a leader, aside from Jesus, who walked the earth and didn't get it wrong at times. Daniel was an incredible young leader and a man full of integrity, but the Bible never mentions that Daniel was a perfect man. There had to be times when Daniel got it wrong. You and I will get it wrong.

Leading today is difficult. With jobs hard to come by and college graduates fighting for fewer jobs, the market is tough. It can be easy, once we get into a position of leadership, to think we have to hold to the lie that leaders don't mess up. A high level of integrity, though, admits mistakes. If you're going to make the shift from conformity to integrity, you're going to have to admit when you give in to an integrity lapse, when you make a wrong call, or when you dishonor someone around you. That's part of making the shift … to admit you are still shifting. Don't buy in to the lie that you have to maintain perfection. Leadership isn't perfection. Leadership is influencing people while we're stumbling to our ultimate destination.

Integrity Means We Walk the Talk

One of the phrases we love to say about people of faith is that they have to "walk the talk," meaning we can't say we believe one thing and act a completely different way. If we as Christians say we love people, but walk around with a snarl and a hard heart, we aren't walking what we're talking. Integrity comes down to a "walk the talk" idea as well. Integrity means that what we do matches what we say and believe. We have to be consistent in how we treat the people around us, how we honor our leaders, how we love our families, and how we serve at our jobs. We can't speak of integrity and leadership but live lives that go against what we say we believe. Integrity in leadership walks what it talks.

One of the fastest ways you and I as young leaders can ruin our integrity is by doing what we say we shouldn't. You see, as a leader, we often have a level of influence and persona that most others don't. To some degree, that's a good thing. Leadership means influence. In order to lead people, you and I have to create that level of influence worth following. Where all of that can go wrong, though, is when we misuse that influence. We

> **LEADERSHIP ISN'T perfection. Leadership is influencing people while we're stumbling to our ultimate destination.**

give up our leadership integrity when we use the influence we've worked hard to gain for selfish reasons. Integrity in leadership means we know how to use our influence. As young leaders of integrity, we make the shift from conforming and just getting what we want to valuing integrity and using our influence for the good of the vision and for others. The young leaders who take the next step up the leadership ladder are the ones who consistently use their gifts, talents, personality, and relationships for the good of the people around them and those who follow them. You don't earn influence by being selfish and you don't keep it by throwing away your integrity.

Integrity Isn't Always Popular

If we return to the story of Daniel in Daniel 6, we get a great idea of just how unpopular integrity can be to the people around us, especially the people who see us as a threat. Daniel went to his upper room to pray. Daniel wasn't causing a scene or publicly insulting the king, he was praying and worshiping his God in private. In Daniel 6:11 and 12, it says, "Then these men went as a group and found Daniel praying and asking God for help. So they went to the king and spoke to him about his royal decree." How did the men find Daniel? It wasn't that he was shouting from the roof that he was disobeying the king, it was his reputation of integrity. These men sought out Daniel that day because they knew he would do what he felt was right. Call it jealousy, payback, or just plain meanness; those men didn't like Daniel and his integrity. As you and I adopt integrity as one of our core values, it's not always going to be popular.

Many of us who have been followers of Christ for a while have experienced the backlash of sticking to what we know is right. My first job was at a grocery store in the town I grew up in. It was one of those summer jobs that teenagers get every year knowing that once school starts again, they'll be long gone from bagging groceries at the checkout line. During my first and only summer at the grocery store, I still remember some fellow employees taking cases of drinks out of the back of the store to their truck one night. In typical high school–pressure fashion, they came and got me, wanting me to participate in what they thought was a brilliant idea. When I got to the back of the store, I told them I wasn't going to join them in their juvenile fun. When they asked why, I simply replied, "It's just not right." Like a scene out of a movie, the three guys I was with began to laugh and mumble under their breath. Once school started back, those guys avoided me for weeks.

When these "integrity-testing" moments happen and people turn their backs on us because we stuck to our guns, it's not our job to necessarily figure out why people will turn on us, but it's our job to be ready to move forward with integrity regardless. As you do so, you may find one of my favorite verses to be a big help. In John 16:33, Jesus says, "I have told you these things, so that in me you may have peace. In this world you will have trouble. But take heart! I have overcome the world."

MAKING THE SHIFT

All truly great leaders have come to a point in their life and leadership where they decide to be people of integrity. You see, as young leaders, we're never going to get ahead or move the organizations and businesses we love forward if we don't have a high level of integrity. The truth is: leadership can be lonely. Alone, you and I are going to have to make the right decision, maintain the same level of excellence, make the tough call, and value people for who they are. We're going to have to shift from being a generation that conforms easily to being a generation that holds tight to integrity.

Realize Integrity's Importance

Making the shift from conformity to integrity begins with believing integrity is important. This may seem like a given to some, but it's not. Integrity is disposable. If it means getting ahead, many see integrity as something they can lay to the side at times. If you and I are going to make the shift, we have to understand integrity must be sustained, not contained only to certain areas of life or work. We have to adopt integrity as a core value to everything we do and say. Integrity must be with us at home, when we're alone, when we're with our team, when we're with our family, and when we're serving others. Integrity isn't just what you're doing when no one else is watching, it's doing right when you have every option in front of you. As future first-chair leaders, we'll often be able to do almost anything we want; *next up* leaders do everything through the lens of integrity. That's what Proverbs 2:20–21 is talking about when it says, "Thus you will walk in the ways of the good and keep to the paths of the righteous. For the upright will live in the land, and the blameless will remain in it." Integrity has lasting and even eternal rewards. Practice it.

Practice to Perfection

In integrity, practice doesn't make perfect. Not any one of us will ever be perfect at this integrity thing. We'll make a shift toward being more consistent with it and valuing it more in our everyday lives, but we'll never get it perfect. What we must do in order to make the shift is practice integrity with an eye on the only One who's ever done it perfectly. When we see the world, others, and what we do through the eyes of Jesus, we become much more inclined to choose integrity over conformity in the situations and problems that present themselves.

You don't earn influence by being selfish, you don't keep it by throwing away your integrity.

Do you remember in Matthew 4 when Jesus was tempted in the desert? Jesus was tempted three times in three completely different ways by Satan. Each time, Jesus reacted in godliness and integrity. Satan will attack our integrity. As you and I make that shift and become leaders in our generation, expect the Enemy's temptation. Look at it all through the eyes of Jesus, who realized His call was far too important to cash in on a little selfish gain. Young leader, your call is important. Make the shift.

> **YOU DON'T earn influence by being selfish, you don't keep it by throwing away your integrity.**

SHIFT SHAPERS

To make the shift from conformity to integrity, you have to believe . . .

1. Integrity begins by leading ourselves.
2. To shift to integrity, we must adopt honesty.
3. Integrity is often the bridge to successful leadership.
4. Leading with integrity requires using our influence rightly.

Integrity isn't just what you're doing when no one is watching, it's doing right when you have every option in front of you. #NextUpBook

#5

FROM *PRIDE* TO HUMILITY

Pride and humility have been in opposition. The fight that rages between pride and humility is one that man has been trying to end since pride entered the world with Adam and Eve. Do you remember why Eve ate the forbidden fruit? Eve took the fruit because she was battling pride. The serpent told her that if she ate of the fruit she would be able to see all that God sees and know all that God knows. Had Eve chosen humility in that moment, she could have resisted the snake's temptation and moved along. Instead, Eve and Adam both ate the fruit because their pride was telling them they wanted to be in the know. Adam and Eve fell because they chose to disobey God. They chose their own pride over God's commands because of what they perceived as benefits from doing so.

While we can never fully reverse what Adam and Eve did that day in the garden, we can make a shift in how we think about ourselves and how we think about others. While we can't do a thing to change the fall of man, we can make a shift so that we fall less often. The leaders who will carry our generation to new heights are going to choose a heart of humility over prideful actions. The young leaders in our best organizations are the ones willing to make the shift.

PRIDE FROM THE FALL

The story of Adam and Eve gives us some great insight on why pride is so bad. Pride, in its truest form, is the thing that creeps its way into our lives and makes us want to believe we're someone we're not. That day in the garden, Eve wanted to be something she was not. Eve wanted to grasp something that wasn't in line with who God created her to be. In a moment, she went from being naked and happy to sewing fig leaves out of embarrassment.

> WHEN WE have a spirit of pride, we are placing what we think of ourselves and what others think of us ahead of what God knows about us.

Pride convinces us that we are our god. When we have a spirit of pride, we are placing what we think of ourselves and what others think of us ahead of what God knows about us. When we allow pride to become central in who we are, the opinions of others and the way others behave toward us become what is most important to us. When pride begins to consume us, we are no longer free to act in what God made us to be. As young leaders, that's a terrible thing. If you and I are more concerned with the opinions of the people we lead, the people we serve, and the people around us than we are with what God has told us, we become inconsistent in our thoughts, ideas, and decisions.

Think back to the last time you learned a secret about someone or maybe you learned how to do something new. What did the pride inside of you want to do with what you learned? It wanted you to elevate yourself and share what you knew. That thing someone told you in confidence suddenly becomes something that will make you appear "in the know." When you brag about that thing you learned to do, it becomes something that grows your pride. In the meantime, we've devalued the people around us by bragging to them or talking about them. Sure, for a short time we appeared to be in the know or have it together, but over the long haul, it's just not worth it. Pride isn't worth the cost and isn't as fulfilling as it advertises. In fact, the Bible says that God opposes the proud. James 4:6 says, "God *opposes the proud* but shows favor to the humble" (emphasis mine). That's one of the scariest verses in all of Scripture! God opposes those who make pride a regular part of their character.

PRIDE FIGHTING

We have to continuously fight to shut pride out of our lives. Several years ago, my wife and I were in Atlanta for a mini-vacation. Atlanta isn't too far from our South Carolina home, so we drove up on a Friday afternoon with plans to take a tour of Turner Field and watch a Braves game before driving back the next day. We went on our tour and then had several hours until the game. Wanting to get to the game pretty early, we decided to stay close to the ballpark and go get a little something to eat. With the help of our "trusty" GPS, we found a restaurant we liked, and we asked for directions. About ten minutes into our journey to the restaurant, we came to a place in busy downtown Atlanta where a road was closed . . . a road our trusty GPS wanted us to take. We drove on by the road and waited for our GPS to reroute us. Several seconds later, the GPS said it had found us another route and we continued on. Several more minutes passed when we came to another wonderful "Road Closed" sign, and then another, and then another. No matter how many times we let our GPS reroute us, we continued to come to closed roads. As frustrating as those signs were when we were hungry, they were there to make sure we didn't go down dangerous roads we weren't prepared to handle.

We have to put up constant "Road Closed" signs when it comes to pride in our lives. Our sinful pride will even try to reroute and try going a different direction to get itself in. We have to adjust and keep closing it down. We have to make a shift in our lives, and it's a constant shifting that's going to get it done. Don't think that by reading the rest of this chapter or by offering up a false sense of humility for a while that you are going to close down pride. It's going to require a fight.

HUMILITY DEFINED

To be humble means we defer and submit to God or someone else. Humility means we don't eat the fruit, say the words, or do the thing that is going to give us a desired result while alienating other people. That's what we as young leaders have to do though. We have to set the example for our peers and for our followers in humility.

We have a perfect example of humility. Philippians 2:6–7 says that Jesus, "Who, being in very nature God, did not consider equality with God something to be used to his own advantage; rather, he made himself nothing by taking the very nature of a servant, being made in human likeness." Did you get that? The very Son of God set the ultimate example in humility when He stepped off His throne and onto earth. That's humility! That's looking out for others above yourself.

Think about the humble acts of Jesus. Jesus was born in a manger when He should have been born in a palace. Jesus lived in everyday robes when He should have been adorned with the fine linen of kings. Jesus served the five thousand when they should have been serving Him. Jesus died for you and me when He should have left

> **WE HAVE to put up constant "Road Closed" signs when it comes to pride in our lives.**

us for dead. Jesus set the example in humility. For leaders, there's never been a better example than the life and leadership of Jesus. He's our example.

Humility Speaks

There's a false belief with a lot of people, especially in the Christian world, that humility means silence. Sure, showing humility can certainly mean we're quiet at times when others wouldn't be, but humility doesn't have to mean we keep our mouths shut. In fact, humility often speaks up. Humility often speaks up in times of trouble for others because we care about their well-being. Humility often means we stand up for what's right because we're tired of seeing the wrong. Humility can mean we speak up for our beliefs. Humility can speak when it casts vision for our organizations. Humility often speaks when pride would be quiet.

One of the greatest ways we as leaders should speak up in humility is when sharing the credit. You see, pride takes all the credit. Pride sits back and fails to speak up about all of the people who had a hand in making something a success. That's poor leadership and does nothing for the morale of our team. Humility, though, speaks up and passes the credit to those who may have been behind the scenes but had a major role in what went right. Humility means we forget about all that we did to make it happen and speak up for those who failed to get recognition.

Leading in humility also means we speak potential into others. This is one of the greatest things that a leader has ever done for me. My parents, my coaches, my pastors—leaders who have spoken up and poured potential into me have helped grow me and my capacity. Pride would have meant they didn't speak that potential because they were looking out for themselves over others. I'm glad that humility isn't silent.

Humility Listens

A year ago, I ran into a friend from college while I was at the grocery store. The friend and I exchanged a few pleasantries and began to talk about our families. I caught him up on what was going on with my family and then asked him about his. Several minutes later, I had to go and went on my way. About three months after running into this person, I coincidently ran into him again. This time, my friend had his daughter by his side. Trying to make conversation with the three-year-old, I asked the little girl where her mom was. The girl immediately dropped her head and then looked up at her dad. My friend put his hand on her shoulder and then went on to remind me that he had told me about his wife leaving them a year before. His wife had moved off and was hours away from her daughter. I felt like a total jerk. I *was* a total jerk. In the midst of my day at the grocery store and talking about my family and myself, I had completely failed to hear him say that his wife had left him. That's pride. Pride doesn't listen when humility knows it should. A person walking in humility and fighting pride knows when someone around them needs a listening ear.

As young leaders, we have to get listening from humility right. When we gain the skill of listening from a place of humility, it greatly improves our leadership potential. When we value listening, no longer do we just want to show off and give our opinion, but we value the feedback of our leaders and peers. We genuinely care about the people we do life with and the people we lead. Humility is willing to listen to those we lead and the people placed around us. Sure, humility speaks, but humility also means we have the knowledge and gauge of when to speak and when to listen. It's a valuable skill that sets *next up* kind of leaders apart.

Humility Is Genuine

One of the most prideful things you and I can do is show false humility. False humility is nothing more than pride with a mask. Think about it: false humility is usually displayed so we can get the benefits that usually accompany a humble person. False humility doesn't care about other people or their well-being—false humility isn't real. As leaders and future first-chair leaders, we have to realize people can see through our disguise. People can see through the false sense of humility we display. If we're leading, we need people who will trust us to get them to their destination. False humility, when seen by those who follow us, does nothing but put up a wall of distrust between us and them. That isn't what we want as leaders. False humility hurts our leadership and our relationships. True humility is genuine and can be seen by those closest to us. True humility doesn't wear a mask and is one of the fastest ways to build trust in those who follow you.

Humility Pays

We should never seek anything from acting in humility. In fact, part of what makes humility genuine and real is that it doesn't seek anything in return. Think about the humility of Jesus. Jesus freely gave everything, including His very life. Humility, though, does have some great benefits. First Peter 5:6 says, "Humble yourselves, therefore, under God's mighty hand, that he may lift you up in due time." The fact that God honors a humble heart displays how gracious and great He really is. Why does God promise to lift us up when we're humble? He tells us humility means we trust Him rather than our own ability to make ourselves great. God honors the humble because He knows the great faith it takes to not speak up in pride when the boss is sitting right in front of you. God honors us when we're humble because He knows that we sacrifice reward when we resist taking all the credit. So He rewards us for our humility instead. Humility pays, but humility doesn't seek return.

MAKING THE SHIFT

Making the shift from pride to humility may be the most time-consuming shift you'll make as a young person or leader. As I mentioned earlier, shifting from a prideful heart to a humble one isn't something you or I can do once and forget about. We have to constantly close the pride road. We won't ever master it, but we can become young leaders who display humility in the way we live our lives and lead our families and organizations.

Know It

If you and I are going to make this shift, we have to know who we are. Pride is often a product of our identity. Pride creeps in most when we forget where we get our worth and we begin to think we have to manufacture it, earn it, or find it in other people. If we're going to make the shift, we have to understand we are nothing without Christ, but we are everything with Him. Romans 5:8 is a well-known but important verse: "But God demonstrates his own love for us in this: While we were still sinners, Christ died for us." We can't read that verse and still think we're somebody in and of ourselves. We also can't read that verse and believe we're nothing with Christ. Christ loves you and me so much that He was willing to lay down His life for our salvation even though we never could have earned it. That's where your worth and identity are found. If we're going to become humble leaders, we have to realize, understand, and believe that we are valuable in Christ alone.

Fight It

Shifting from pride to humility means we constantly fight to stay humble. As I mentioned earlier, we'll never get it perfect or come to a place where we can put the fight on the back burner. Staying humble is like staying fit. I'm one of those people who loves to eat. I love to eat, but I'm not a huge fan of exercise. So staying fit and keeping my weight down is a fight I do battle with every day. Every day I wake up, I'm faced with the decision of eating well or eating junk. I'm faced with the decision to go for a run or watch television. It's a constant fight in my mind and in my body. That's what shifting to humility is like too. Every day, we have to choose to make the right decisions when it comes to acting in a humble way.

Filter It

One of the things I have found most helpful in shifting from pride to humility is recognizing pride spots in my life and filtering them out. What I mean is when those places come up where I tend to speak out or act out in pride, I make it a priority to recognize them. When I recognize those spots, I can run them through the filter in my head of "Am I going to say this just to make myself look good?" If my filter tells me it's out of pride, I try my best to stay quiet instead. Those spots where I could brag or easily steal the credit because the people who helped me aren't in the room, I run them through my pride filter. If there's a situation where I may even have to hold back something good because I'm saying it out of pride, I filter that stuff out as well. If you're going to make the shift from being a person of pride to humility, you're going to have to find a way to shift your mindset and filter your prideful thoughts. It's important that you and I make an effort and make a way to practice humility. Humility is one of God's favorite characteristics and one of a leader's greatest tools.

SHIFT SHAPERS

To make the shift from pride to humility, you have to believe . . .

1. I must fight against pride all day, every day.
2. I am somebody because of Christ, not my own doing.
3. Humility has rewards that pride can never offer.

Pride isn't just elevating self, it's devaluing others because of how you feel about self. Fight it! #NextUpBook

#6

FROM *PASSIVE* TO PASSIONATE

What's that one thing that sets great leaders apart from other leaders? That one factor that makes us look at someone and think, "They just have something not many people have"?

I think it is passion. A passionate leader can turn the organization they serve into a powerhouse of their field. A passionate leader has the ability to turn even the toughest followers into dedicated and flourishing members of the team. On the other hand, a person who is passive in their feelings toward what they are doing and the organization they are leading can suck the momentum out of their organization and the people around them very quickly. Passive people are in a place to get by and draw a paycheck. The passive people in our generation feel entitled to be where they are and don't show the passion to get to where they need to be. The difference passion can make in our leadership is the difference between moving our organizations ahead to the next level and having them flame out after the current senior leader passes the torch.

PASSIVE OR PASSION?

There's a story Jesus tells in Scripture that better illustrates a passive attitude than any story I could tell. In Luke 10, Jesus talks about a man who was walking down the road to Jericho. This guy wasn't that much different from you and me, he was just someone making a trip into town on an average day. This man was walking along the road when some guys came from out of nowhere and jumped him. The robbers cleaned him of his wallet and money, and beat him up. Once they did all the damage they could do, they left him for dead.

As the guy lay on the side of the road, bloody and bruised, he looked up and noticed a priest walking toward him. Now, I have to think this guy was thrilled at the sight of a priest. Well, his hope dimmed as the priest walked right past him, leaving him on the side of the road. Not long after, another guy walked down the road, saw the beaten man, and strolled right on past.

> PASSION IS the recognition that something has to be done and this "something" can be done by us. Passive is carrying on our way without recognizing the opportunities in front of us.

A little while later, a common, everyday Samaritan guy walked down the road toward the desperate man. At this point, I have to think he was lying there, looking through blood and tears, and thinking his situation is hopeless. He had to have been thinking, "If the priest wasn't stopping and the other guy ignored me, this third person isn't going to have a thing to do with me." Yet as the Samaritan reached the beaten man, he stopped, stooped down, and began to patch his wounds. He took the poor guy to the inn and told the innkeeper to give him whatever he needed. He paid the bill.

You see, that story illustrates two kinds of people. On one hand, we have the priest and the second guy (a Levite) who are completely passive about the situation. Those two had an opportunity to do something great but chose to just get to their next place. Then you have the common man, a Samaritan, who decides he's going to do something about what he sees in front of him. He sees the guy in need and it brings about a passion inside of him to do something about it. He even goes above and beyond to help the robbed man because he is passionate about his need. That's the difference between passive and passionate. Passion is the recognition that something has to be done and this "something" can be done by us. Passive is carrying on our way without recognizing the opportunities in front of us.

PASSIVE IN LEADERSHIP

One of the greatest contributors to passive living and leadership is being a people-pleaser. I really like to be liked. I want the people around me to enjoy spending time with me. I want the people who lead me and the people I lead to be happy with me and enjoy being a part of the same team. This can often lead to the struggle to let things pass by me that I shouldn't. Those little things that need our attention now, when allowed to pass on by, can be big things later. Better yet, those little ideas we have about the future now could pay huge dividends in the future. Sometimes, we don't capitalize on those ideas because we're afraid we'll alienate or upset the people involved in them now. Those of us who lead in the church understand this. We allow the same programs to go unchanged because we're afraid to have a tough conversation with the person who's been leading it for years. Or, better yet, we let someone continue to operate in a ministry or place where they aren't gifted because we're afraid of the tough conversation. Do we need to respect people and their feelings? Absolutely—there's no great leader who doesn't. Do we need to capitalize on the ideas and thoughts that God puts into our heads and hearts? Definitely. We can't be afraid to step out and step up to a great idea. We have to take action even though we know it may cost us something. Some of history's greatest ideas have been left in a Moleskine journal or on a conference room's whiteboard.

One of my vivid memories from my teenage years is when I was a new driver and went out with some friends on a Friday afternoon. We were driving around, looking for something to do, when we came to a long, straight, back road not too far from one of my friend's houses. We found something to do. I stopped my car, put the car in neutral, and pressed the accelerator. Once the accelerator was pressed, I popped the car into drive. What it caused was squealing tires and black marks in the road. As teenagers, we thought this was greatest thing ever. We went back to that long, straight road all summer long. I guess that poor Grand Am deserved to be a little unreliable.

What we were doing was creating friction with our tires on the road. The reason we heard squealing sounds and saw black marks behind us was because of the friction under the tires when we popped the car into drive. That's what happens when we, as young people and leaders, begin to move forward with our lives and with what we're leading. Forward movement creates friction. When we're more concerned about pleasing people and avoiding friction, we become passive and lack the passion needed to succeed. We can't be afraid of friction. Now, don't get me wrong, we shouldn't go around and create friction for the sake of it in an attempt to make us feel like we're moving forward. That's careless. We can't, though, let our fear of friction with others prevent us from moving forward.

PASSION IS CRUCIAL

One of my favorite moments in all of Scripture is Pentecost. I can always imagine the sights and sounds of that holy and monumental day when I read about it. It was seemingly like most other days when, out of nowhere, came loud sounds and strong winds that filled the entire house where the disciples were. They saw some crazy things, were filled with the Holy Spirit, and began to speak in tongues. As the racket ensued, crowds heard what was going on and began to gather around the house. The crowd couldn't quite put together all that was happening, so they began to speculate that maybe the disciples were drunk.

I love what happens next in the story. Peter and the other disciples stood up and addressed the crowd. At that point, Peter goes into what has to be the second greatest sermon in the history of the world (behind the Sermon on the Mount, of course). After Peter gets done with his sermon, the Bible says in Acts 2:47, "The Lord added to their number daily those who were being saved." You see, passion has its rewards. Peter could have chosen to sit idly by when the crowd gathered around and started accusing him of sipping the sauce. Instead, he stood up and began a passionate movement. That's what's possible when a leader is passionate and allows his passion to spill out. That's what happens when we put people-pleasing on a back burner and bring godly passion to the front.

Our passion comes out when we show intense feeling or excitement about something. Our passion comes through when we believe in and care about what we're doing. As young people, passion is one of our greatest assets. Where we as young leaders lack in life experience, we make up for in young passion. Where we as inexperienced leaders lack in wisdom, we make up for in unbridled passion. Where we lack in influence, we can make up for in passion. We have to use the advantage of passion as we serve, lead, and are led where we serve. Being young and having fewer opportunities for life to get the best of us, we are blessed with a great ability to have passion and to chase what we're passionate about. We have to take advantage of this.

> SOME OF history's greatest ideas have been left in a Moleskine journal or on a conference room's whiteboard.

I love fireworks. Here in the great state of South Carolina, we can still buy and shoot fireworks on our own in most places. It really is a great advantage of living in the South. Every Fourth of July for the last couple of years, my wife and I have teamed up with a few other couples and made our own fireworks show.

Every year, as we're purchasing our fireworks, we undoubtedly stumble upon a fireworks stand that has a special where we can buy a certain amount of fireworks and get a couple rolls of 1,000 firecrackers for free. We don't much care for hearing a bunch of noise, but we always take the firecrackers and light them anyway. The nice thing is, we don't have to light 1,000 firecrackers. Instead, each firecracker is tied to the one beside it so it creates a continuous chain that passes the light from one to the next. So, you can light a strand of 1,000 firecrackers with one single match. That's how passion operates in our lives. One person who's passionate about what they're doing can become a leader. One leader who is passionate about the cause they represent can change their organization and the world. It all starts with one passionate light.

PASSION IS A LEADERSHIP SYNONYM

Leadership is certainly more than passion. After all, there are plenty of passionate people who aren't called to be leaders. There are passionate people everywhere who will never be a *next up* leader or be called to lead a cause, organization, or even a family. Passion is, though, the fuel that powers leadership. Passion is the thing all great leaders have inside of them that inspires them to get up in the morning. Passion is the fuel that drives a leader to work through the problems and roadblocks that are seen in front of them. Passion is the thing that causes leaders to push past when everyone else gives in. Passion powers us. Passion is what causes people like Peter to begin movements and start revolutions. It's all because of passion.

A leader's passion comes from the heart. The cardiovascular system is vitally important to the human body. I'm no doctor,

> **PASSION IS the fuel that drives a leader to work through the problems and roadblocks that are seen in front of them. Passion is the thing that causes leaders to push past when everyone else gives in.**

but I have a pretty good idea that without my heart, veins, arteries, or blood, I'd be a goner. Without my cardiovascular system, I would cease to exist. It's no wonder the heart is often pictured as the home for the soul of a human being. The heart is that place deep inside each of us that believes for things, hopes for the best, dreams of significance, loves deeply, and desires greatness. Real passion, the passion it takes to be a *next up* leader and lead movements, comes from deep within us and isn't easily quenched. That's passion. That's leadership.

PASSION CAUSES ACTION

If passion is the fuel of leadership, acting on that passion is the accelerator. Inside my car, I usually have at least a quarter tank of fuel. So I usually have the potential to drive a couple of hundred miles at any time I choose. Without a gas pedal, though, I'll never be able to use the fuel I paid too much for at the pump. That's the way it is with our passion. We have to put our passion to action by allowing it to move us to do something. Remember back to the story Jesus told about the Good Samaritan. The Good Samaritan didn't just look on the beat-up guy and have compassion—he used that passion and acted on it.

Real passion, the kind of passion that comes from the heart, can't exist and not move us to action. Real passion is the thing that moves us from making statements like, "Man, I wish something would change here," to making statements like, "I'm doing something to change this." That's passion in action. It's not just seeing the need, but meeting the need. It's not just recognizing things aren't as they should be, it is helping make them as they should be.

Passion Propels

A young leader with passion not only propels herself forward and up the organizational ladder, she propels her cause forward as well. Passion is the very thing that is going to help the world become a better place. Passion propels a young leader forward with her senior management, but it also propels the leader forward when things get tough. If we were to talk about passion and not mention the fact that it isn't always easy, we would miss a major point. Passion causes conflict. Passion will waver. Passion, though, will propel you through it all.

Passion Passes

I'm a self-diagnosed germaphobe. Now, before you accuse me of being insensitive to the actually diagnosed germaphobes across the world, hear me out. Several weeks ago I was making my way back from Kentucky. We were on the last leg of the flight and there was an empty seat between me and the other person in my row. Like all other flyers, we were hoping, as time got close for the cabin door to be shut, that we'd be blessed with that empty seat and a little more room. As often happens, however, seconds before the cabin door shut, a guy in his early twenties made his way down the aisle. I politely got up so he could crawl in and have a seat. About two or three minutes after sitting down, I began to hear this guy grunt under his breath and begin sniffing like his nose was running. As I watched him get a tissue out from his pocket, I knew I was in for a *long* short flight.

What I know about germs is that they pass from one person to another. That's why, on any given Sunday morning at church, I sanitize my hands about ten times. I'm a germaphobe because I know germs pass from person to person, and when they pass, I get sick.

Passion also infects the people around us. It's so much better than passing germs because passion has the chance to drastically improve the lives of those who catch it. A good leader maintains their passion but passes it along to the people around them as well. It fuels the people around them and the people they lead until they gain the same passion. Like firecrackers in a stand or germs on a plane, we need to learn to pass the passion.

Passion Promotes

Passion promotes momentum in the organization you serve in and might one day lead. When a leader in any organization, church, non-profit, or group becomes passionate about the vision and mission of the organization, it has the power to promote momentum throughout. As young leaders, we have a great ability to build momentum. Being young, we're willing to go to new lengths, show new ideas, bring new perspectives, and have fresh vision that can promote momentum in our organizations. As young leaders and being much newer to our organization, we're often left without some of the culture of the past that many of the people around us have in them. This has its setbacks, of course, but being new to the organization and not being able to see past failures and successes also allows us to promote new ideas and build new, more powerful momentum.

MAKING THE SHIFT

Making the shift from passive to passionate is one we have to make quickly. The truth is, if you're a young person who is passive about the very things you claim matter to you, you may never be a *next up* leader. However, if you're fighting to keep your passion or turn up your passion for the people you serve and the cause you believe in, you can make the shift. There should be a sense of urgency, but you can shift from feeling like you're falling into passive living and leadership to being fired up with passion.

Stoke the Flame

About a year ago, I began to feel my passion turning to passivity. I didn't get as excited as I used to about the things that really mattered, and when I felt like I did get excited, it wore me out. Even though I'm young in life experience and leadership, I knew it wasn't right. Thankfully, a mentor of mine reminded me I had to stoke the passion flame. Just like a real fire has to be stoked and have new wood added, our passion has to be maintained as well. It's important that you and I now, even as young people, realize the importance of downtime and getting away. I know the temptation. The temptation here is that we can do that later because right now we have to work harder than everyone else to prove we're worthy of being next or worthy of staying in our current position. Yes, work hard; don't use this as an excuse to fall victim to our entitled and lazy generational tendencies. Do, though, make sure you stoke your passion flame. Whatever it takes to fill you up with energy and revive your spirit, do it. Make it a practice. If passion is your fuel, you've got to visit the gas station from time to time to get some more.

Guard Your Passion

We all have those one or two people in our lives who seemingly always need something of us whenever we're around them. These people's problems always get worse and worse, and they always need a hand up or a handout. These people suck the life out of us. I understand that much like the Good Samaritan, we have to love people and care for people, even when it's hard. We have to be willing to give a hand up to the people around us who need our attention. The people we have to guard against, though, are the ones who don't want help but just want more problems. These are the people who, despite asking for your advice about their finances, choose to continue with the same spending habits, or they ask for relationship advice but always return to the same destructive relationship. These are the people who enjoy talking about their own problems and the problems of others. Negative and problem-seeking people seem to look for someone they can communicate with who seems to have life together. They don't necessarily care about pulling themselves up, but just want to suck some hope from someone around them. Don't let those people suck the passion out of you. Don't lend your ear to those people any more than you have to. Their negativity and hopelessness will do nothing but put a lid on your passion. Guard it.

Return to Your Purpose

Mary Magdalene and Mary the mother of James were on their way to anoint the body of Jesus not long after He had been placed in the tomb. When they got to the tomb, the stone had been rolled away. Jesus appeared first to Mary Magdalene after rising from the dead. Mary, being passionate about Jesus, went to tell everyone she could about Jesus not being in the tomb any longer. No one believed her. The disciples didn't even believe Mary when she told them Jesus had risen from the grave. Later, Jesus appears before the disciples and rebukes them for their unbelief. The disciples had forgotten their real calling and their real purpose. They had been told about the resurrection, but had still refused to believe. After scolding the disciples, Jesus gave them their purpose. In Mark 16:15, Jesus tells the disciples, "Go into all the world and preach the gospel to all creation." That was the disciples' purpose.

In the midst of their unbelief, Jesus reminded them they were part of something much bigger than themselves. We have to remind ourselves of the same. That's where passion comes from. That's how we keep passion in our lives and leadership alive!

SHIFT SHAPERS

To make the shift from passive to passionate, you have to believe . . .

1. Passion is a young leader's most valuable asset.
2. To spread passion, we have to stoke the flame in our own lives.
3. Our passion has to be great because our purpose is great.

Passion turns statements like, "Someone could . . ." to "I just have to." Don't underestimate a passionate person. #NextUpBook

#7

FROM *SELFISHNESS* TO LOVE

"I love you . . ."
"I love that shirt . . ."
"I love this band . . ."
"I love that food . . ."
"I love my job . . ."

Love is one of our society's most misunderstood and most overused words. We've become a generation and a society that has so confused the meaning of love, we often forget what it means entirely. Love means we constantly care for someone. Can we love someone? Yes. Can we love God? Yes. Can we love more than one person? Yes. Love, in its simplest and most stripped-down form, means we care about someone else so deeply that we're willing to act differently because of it.

Selfishness is one of our most overlooked bad habits as a generation. In fact, we often dismiss our own selfishness and blame it on those around us. We think other people don't deserve our giving or our love, so we keep it to ourselves and refuse to give anything good to those around us. Selfishness, while easy to dismiss and excuse, can be a big hindrance to a leader. Selfishness puts up an unnecessary wall between people, and it leads to distrust and failed initiatives.

SELFISHNESS SHOWS

One day, Jesus was out walking around, moving from place to place, when a young man stopped Him to ask a question. The young man asked Jesus what he had to do in order to spend eternity in heaven. Knowing that the young man already had a good grasp on it, Jesus told him all he had to do was keep the commands that had been given to him. Trying to narrow it down some, the young man asked Jesus which commands exactly He was talking about. Jesus looked at the young guy and told him, "You shall not murder, you shall not commit adultery, you shall not steal, you shall not give false testimony, honor your father and mother, and love your neighbor as yourself" (Matthew 19:18–19). Having heard Jesus' response, I can imagine the young man got really excited and said, "I've done all of that. I've got this. I'm good to go!" Just as the young man was about to walk away filled with pride in his own accomplishments, Jesus said, "If you want to be perfect, go, sell your possessions and give to the poor, and you will have treasure in heaven. Then come, follow me" (v. 21). The story ends in verse 22 with the words, "When the young man heard this, he went away sad, because he had great wealth."

The story of the rich young ruler in Matthew 19 is one of my favorite stories in the New Testament. Not because it gives me incredible hope or encourages me when life has me down but because it serves as a great reminder that following rules isn't all there is to life, and selfishness can cause us to miss out on the very essence of life. The young man in the story was so selfish with what he owned that he refused to give it up in order to follow the very Life-Giver Himself. Can you imagine how the story would have ended differently had the rich young man been willing to abandon his selfishness and follow Jesus with all he had? Maybe he would have gone on to be one of Christianity's greatest leaders—we'll never really know. Matthew would have written about this man in a completely different light. Selfishness caused the young man to miss out on some incredible opportunities.

Selfishness means we only care about ourselves. How many times have you heard on the news or seen in a magazine or read in a blog that our generation is only concerned with ourselves? I'm afraid everyone is right. I'm afraid that not just our generation but society as a whole has become very self-absorbed. If we're going to become the next leaders of our organizations, our churches, our businesses, and our families, we're going to have to learn to be concerned with others. If we don't, we're going to miss out on the world of opportunity that potentially awaits us. If we don't, we're going to fail in moving forward.

> **IF WE'RE thinking of leading in the present or the future, we're going to have to know what it's like to shift from being people concerned with hoarding our blessings and become people willing to love our peers.**

Unfortunately, selfishness is an easy response. Selfishness can play its way into every part of our lives. We can be selfish with our money and refuse to give any of it to others in need. We can be selfish with our time. We can be selfish with our stuff. Selfishness can take over our lives.

Often times, we become selfish because we fail to be thankful. When we're truly thankful for what we have or what's been given to us, we're naturally giving and loving. You see, thankfulness often comes when we recognize that what we have hasn't always been and doesn't always have to be. You're more thankful for a home when you know what it's like not to have one. You're more thankful for food when you can think of a time when you were hungry. You're more thankful for grace when you know what it was like to get what you deserved. Thankfulness wells up inside of us and encourages us to give to others so they can feel the same things we're able to feel. Thankfulness overcomes selfishness.

Matthew 16:25 says, "For whoever wants to save their life will lose it, but whoever loses their life for me will find it." Did you catch that? Not only is selfishness bad for our society, but it can be bad for our eternity. Just like the rich young man, refusing to be a loving and giving person can literally change our lives. We have to make the shift. If we're thinking of leading in the present or the future, we're going to have to know what it's like to shift from being people concerned with hoarding our blessings and become people willing to love our peers.

A LOOK AT LOVE

Mark 14 gives us a beautiful picture of love. Not only does it feature a selfless person, it also sheds light on what Jesus Himself thought about love. In Mark 14, a woman named Mary came to Jesus with a jar of extremely expensive perfume. Understanding who Jesus was and loving Him deeply, the lady broke the jar and began to pour the expensive perfume on Jesus' head. Other people who were standing around didn't appreciate her using all the perfume on Jesus and began to grumble about how much she had wasted what was really valuable. They began to talk about all that Mary could have done with the perfume rather than dumping it out. As the people started to get loud, Jesus stopped the chatter and said, "Why are you bothering her? She has done a beautiful thing to me. . . . She did what she could. She poured perfume on my body beforehand to prepare for my burial. Truly I tell you, wherever the gospel is preached throughout the world, what she has done will also be told, in memory of her" (Mark 14:6, 8–9). Did you catch that? Jesus acknowledges Mary's sacrifice and lack of selfishness and commends her on her love for Him. That's what love is really all about. Love isn't about liking something a lot or just about loving our special someone, love is about being selfless and giving up what is valuable so that someone else can be blessed. The fact is, we can all look at Mary and see an example of love. We can look at Mary and see what it looks like when we've shifted from selfishness to love for our Savior.

In Luke 10, some teachers of the religious law come to Jesus and ask Him about the most important commandment in the Bible. Realizing they are trying to catch Him in a game of playing favorites, Jesus responds with, "'Love the Lord your God with all your heart and with all your soul and with all your strength and with all your mind'; and 'Love your neighbor as yourself'" (Luke 10:27). It is so important for us to love not only God but the people around us. The people we like and the people we dislike. The people we follow and the people who follow us. The people we know and the people we meet for the first time. Love is important. Love changes things.

LOVE MOVES

As leaders, no matter where we are on the ladder, it's important for us to shift to love. As we grow in influence and leadership position, love will be the thing that often helps us move forward and treat people in a respectable manner. The truth is: love is more than just a saying, a word, or even a verse of Scripture. We could spend the next three hundred pages on stories about love and Bible stories proving God's love and how we should follow it. At the end of the day, however, love has to move. Love has to move you and me to do something beyond "talk."

Love Sacrifices

We don't have to think very long before we can come up with a great example of how love sacrifices. Jesus is our obvious example of sacrificial love. While it may seem obvious and even elementary to talk about the love of Jesus and its sacrificial nature, we need to be reminded of what genuine love looks like. Do you remember what happened right after Jesus was baptized in Matthew 3? Right after we get this spectacular picture of Jesus going under the water and rising out of it and the heavens opening up, we see in the very next chapter that Jesus was led by the Spirit into the wilderness to be tempted. Jesus fasted for forty days, and that's when Satan came and hit Jesus with temptation's big guns. Satan came to Jesus three times, trying to convince Jesus to give up this entire idea of sacrificing Himself for the sins of the world. Satan gave Jesus an easy out, three times, but He didn't take it.

Knowing what was to come over the next few years, Jesus still resisted the temptation. They weren't just little temptations either; Satan offered Jesus some pretty big things. Jesus sacrificed them all so He could be sacrificed for us. That's what love does. Love gives up what it could have and gives away what it doesn't have to. Don't think Jesus is the only one who is supposed to sacrifice either. In John 15:13, Jesus Himself says, "Greater love has no one than this: to lay down one's life for one's friends." Jesus expects us to sacrifice for the people around us as well. No, it probably won't be your life, but it may be something you love or something that's tough to give up. If we're going to be the kind of leaders who are trusted with the future, we're going to have to learn to sacrifice.

Love Hides

Love doesn't seek attention. In fact, real love is often behind the scenes. Many times, as leaders, we'll stand in the gap for people and give things up for people, and they'll never find out about it. That's the nature of leadership. As a leader, people will confide in you, and you often know about situations before they become public knowledge. Great leaders serve the people around them by protecting their people. People under your leadership may never know how you've protected them, but love says you do it anyway.

One of the greatest examples of love hiding is found in my mother. Growing up, my mom would constantly do things for me, give things to me, and sacrifice her wants for me. She never expected credit for those things. Mom never put a sticker on my new jeans that said, "I bought these instead of the shirt I wanted for myself." She didn't do that because that's not love. Love doesn't demand a pat on the back or public recognition. Love others because you care about them, not because you want recognition for anything. Love others for the cause of your organization, not for the credit.

Love Connects

When I was a senior in high school, something tragic happened only days before Christmas. I was asleep in my bed one night when the phone by my pillow began to vibrate. Barely waking up, and thinking that the vibration was nothing, I went back to sleep and ignored the disruption. Only seconds later, my phone did the same thing. Being a little more awake this time, I picked up the phone and noticed a good friend of mine was calling. That was when my Christmas suddenly changed. On the other end of the phone was my friend telling me that my best friend had just been in a car accident and was dead on the scene. This was a friend I had known all of my life—the guy I had gone to kindergarten with, had played Little League baseball with, and had learned to drive with. Just like that, he was gone.

After getting the phone call, I got up and made my way to his parents' house. As morning came, people began to flood my friend's parents' house with phone calls and flowers. For the next few months, there was hardly ever a time when someone wasn't visiting his parents or sending them food or gifts. Even after his death, my friend connected with people. He was leading and didn't even know it. He was leading because he loved people. People loved him because they felt connected to him when he knew their name the first time after meeting them and always made a point after that to speak to them when he saw them. He connected. He was a good leader.

Love Reveals

All good parents understand the importance of speaking truth to their children, even when the truth hurts. Why do parents sometimes try to keep their children from making mistakes?

Why do parents sometimes correct their children when they're wrong? Parents are willing to reveal the truth because they love their children. You see, real love speaks truth, even when it's tough truth. I experience tough love just about every time I go to a certain Mexican restaurant in our small city that uses a lot of fresh ingredients in their salsa. While I love the salsa, it often has large pieces of cilantro mixed into it. On more than one occasion, I've gone to this restaurant for lunch and gone back to work without checking my teeth. It never fails, though, someone always stops me not long after I get back to the office and tells me I have something in my teeth. Those people love me. It takes love to reveal the tough truth . . . no matter how trivial it may seem. At the same time, though, real love reveals truth but covers it in grace. We can be gracious and truthful at the same time.

For us as young leaders, we're going to have to learn what it's like to speak the truth out of love. In case you haven't noticed, not everyone thinks the same way you do and reacts to situations the same way you do. Not everyone understands things quite like you. We have to get good at correcting people and calling people out on their wrong behavior while being gracious in the process. And we have to be willing to be corrected ourselves.

Love Empowers

My first paying job in ministry was offered to me by a guy who had just become a pastor again after taking a long break doing sales at a jewelry store. While he was still new to the church he was pastoring, he believed his church needed a part-time youth pastor to care for the students, and he believed I needed a solid start in paid ministry. He called me my junior year of college and asked me if I'd be interested. Being in college and having little to no money, I was willing to take just about anything if it meant the ramen noodles could stay out of my mouth for a little while. I traveled an hour or so up the road to be interviewed by the committee at the church and was hired a week or so later. I drove that hour a few times a week for almost two full years. During those two years, my youth group grew, but not drastically. The church grew, but not drastically. Instead of seeing extreme numerical growth in attendance, I saw extreme growth in myself. You see, that pastor empowered me to be more than I thought I could be. He believed in an unproven, ungraduated, and untrained boy and hired him to work alongside him at a church he was still getting used to. That pastor looked past my faults and looked into my potential. He looked through my present and saw what could be. He breathed life and hope into me. He taught me. He fed me and prayed for me. He empowered me.

That's what leaders do for those they lead. They empower others and, in the process, lead them to do things they never thought possible. A couple of years ago, that pastor went to be with Jesus. What he left behind was a young man who felt called to change the world. That's the love Jesus had in mind.

Love Covers

Those of us who were raised in church or have spent some time studying or reading the Bible have probably heard 1 Peter 4:8, "Above all, love each other deeply, because love covers over a multitude of sins." As leaders of love, we don't have to worry about a key team member leaving for a more attractive job, because we want what's best for them. When love drives our leadership, we don't have to dread what's ahead; we can look forward to conversations about the future with people we enjoy and care about. The people you lead and the people around you will cause far fewer problems when they know you love them. Even though some people may disagree with you and voice that disagreement, when they know you love them, they'll do it in such a better way than they would if you didn't.

> AT THE END of the day, leadership without love is just careful manipulation.

As a leader, we want to be around people who will call us out when they strongly disagree with something we're doing. We want people around us who will come to us when they believe we're making a mistake or going in the wrong direction. When those people have experienced our love, they'll do that with grace and in a way that builds us up.

MAKING THE SHIFT

Not a single person reading this is a stranger to loving others. We all know what it's like to love those around us. At the same time, no one reading this is exempt from being selfish at times in their life and while they're leading. What the great leaders learn to do is eventually have more moments of love than moments of selfishness. The people who lead movements and change the world are the ones who make the shift to show love in more situations and selfishness in less. A *next up* leader is one who learns to make the shift from being selfish with what they have to loving others enough to give some of it up.

Know You Are Loved

The first thing you and I have to do in order to love others more? We have to realize how much *we're* loved. You and I are loved by the Creator of the world Himself. We're loved by the One who created everything we see, everything we smell, everything we feel, and everything we are. He loves us so much, in fact, that it meant sacrificing His only Son so we could be with Him. When we begin to understand that and keep God's love at the front of our thoughts and life, we can begin to love others more. There's something about knowing we're loved that makes us more sacrificial, more generous, more gracious, and more loving. Understand and never forget that you are loved.

Know Yourself

We all have those places in our lives where selfishness comes a little easier. Maybe it's something in our past or a lack of something in our past that causes us to hold on to certain things a little tighter than others. If we're going to shift from selfishness to love, we have to understand those areas in our life where we're most prone to being selfish. Only when we identify those areas, whether it be with our money, our stuff, our time, our ideas, can we begin to shift toward loving others without restraint or obstacles.

Know Your Leadership

At the end of the day, leadership without love is just careful manipulation. When you and I take the love aspect out of anything we do, our actions lose much of their worth. Can we move people toward a goal without love? Sure. Can we help people become all that they are designed to be and could be without loving them? No. It takes love to lead people to do more. That's what a *next up* leader does. It isn't just about the bottom line or attendance numbers, it's about the lives of the people we lead. It's about investing in the people beside us in the cause we champion. Know what kind of leader you want to be. Choose loving over manipulating.

SHIFT SHAPERS

To make the shift from selfishness to love, you have to believe . . .

1. Love is so much more than a strong like or empty words; love moves.
2. The love that we receive allows us to know how to love others.
3. Real leadership isn't manipulation; it's influence through love.

Real leadership is influence through love. #NextUpBook

#8

FROM *PREMATURE* TO PATIENT

For transparency's sake, I have to say that I'm not very good at being patient. I'm one of those people who finds himself constantly thinking about schedules and what's coming up next. I don't like lines at the grocery store or the drugstore or at the pretzel store in the mall. I often find myself leaving functions early because I've lost patience with their length. I can't sit still very long on a lazy Saturday afternoon because my patience and activity clock begin to run down.

My confessions aside, though, patience is something I've gotten better at over time. Maybe lines still make me sick and the idea of waiting for something often causes my anger meter to skyrocket, but I have learned a little over the last few years. I've gotten better with waiting in line, waiting for things, and waiting for people. I'm making the shift from running short on patience with the people around me and the things that happen to me to being a person who is willing to take things as they come. I've learned some stuff along the way. I've learned what it means to care for people even though they mess up what I just tried to teach them. I've learned that some of the best things in life aren't immediately available. I've become a more patient leader and person. I'm still shifting, but I'm moving.

LIVING AND LEADING AHEAD OF TIME

Merriam-Webster says that premature means "Happening too soon or earlier than usual."[2] I love this definition because that's exactly what happens when we as leaders begin to lose patience and do things prematurely—we make it happen too soon. Our generation didn't accidentally get our lack of patience and desire for things to happen immediately. After all, I can't think of a time my family didn't have a microwave and a toaster oven. Those two appliances are meant to get things done quickly and provide instantaneous results. Most of us have phones in our pockets that can access just about any information as soon as we want it (go ahead, send that tweet and then continue reading, we'll still be here). From social networking to search engines to DVR to microwaves and toasters, we have been conditioned to make things happen immediately . . . to have things when we want them.

Because of our conditioning to have things happen quickly, we've become so accustomed to having things our way, the "right" way, that we've let our premature attitude seep into every other part of our lives. We want people to immediately understand what we're teaching them. We want them to become perfect at it overnight. We want our relationship with God to grow quickly. We want the relationships we form to escalate quickly to a place it should really take us years to get to. We want the people who lead us and the people we lead to buy in to what we're trying to sell them the second we get it out of our mouths. We want it our way, right away. We got that way honestly, but that doesn't mean it's right. In fact, wanting immediate results is often wrong and unreasonable. What we're left with at the end of the day is a lot of frustration and pent-up anger.

THE REASON FOR BEING PREMATURE

I can't begin to tell you how many times I've had this thought as a young person in my twenties. The thought goes something like, "I've got to get out of here *now*. If I don't, I'm gonna be here forever!" You see, at my age, what I see and where I am is often all I can think of. Instead of thinking about what could happen down the road or what could happen between now and the time I get somewhere else, I immediately think what I see is all there is. That works for short, passionate bursts when I'm excited about something, but it doesn't bode well for long-term leadership. What happens during all of my frustration is I jump at things prematurely or I give up prematurely. I get too impatient and too concerned with the end result that I forget about the process in between.

My wife loves to cook, especially at Christmas. In fact, every Christmas she sets aside time to bake some goodies and try some new recipes. This past Christmas, she decided she was going to try her hand at a double-layer cheesecake. The picture looked tremendous. This cheesecake was going to be the Christmas baking item of the century!

As baking day came, we went to the grocery store and got the ingredients for the cheesecake. We spent much of that Saturday in the kitchen together. I helped her stir while she mixed. I set oven timers and kept my eye on the cheesecake layers so it wouldn't begin to sag in the middle while it was still cooking.

As the timer for the final cheesecake layer went off, I was

excited, to say the least. The kitchen timer, normally a very annoying sound, was like angels singing. I jumped up from the recliner and ran into the kitchen to help Melissa get the layers out of the oven. As I ran up to the oven, I slipped and fell in some water that we had gotten on the floor earlier in the day. I did some serious damage. The repercussions of my fall made the middle of the cheesecake cave in. You see, that's what happens when we get so caught up in the end result and what could happen down the road. We focus so much on the desired result that we make mistakes in the process. We make premature decisions and conclusions, and we fall in the process. We have to begin to shift. We have to become people and leaders who understand the importance of not overlooking the process while trying to get an end result.

PATIENCE: NOT JUST A VIRTUE, A NECESSITY

I love my family. However, neither my immediate family nor Melissa's immediate family live very close to our home. When our parents come to visit us, they never know exactly where they're going because they've never lived in our town before. The last time my in-laws were in town, we decided to go out to eat. My in-laws followed us in their car to the restaurant.

Where we were going to eat wasn't but about ten minutes away. However, on the way, there were several red lights and turns. The first stoplight we came to was yellow. For a split second, I thought about doing what I normally do in that situation, hit the gas and speed through just in time. Just as I was about to punch the accelerator, though, I remembered that my in-laws were behind me and probably wouldn't know where to go if I left them, so I hit the brake instead. After the light turned green, we drove on and came to a left turn. In a small break of cars coming, I started to roll out to make the turn. Just before I started to turn, I remembered that my in-laws were behind me and didn't know the way to the restaurant. I waited until there was space for both of us to turn before going. You see, even though I enjoy getting places fast and early, I understand that sometimes, we have to show patience so those around us

> **THAT'S WHAT** happens when we get so caught up in the end result and what could happen down the road. We focus so much on the desired result that we make mistakes in the process.

don't get lost along the way. If I would have stomped the gas when the light turned yellow or made the turn at the first small break in traffic, I would have gotten to my destination, but I would have gotten there alone ... without the ones following me.

As *next up* young leaders, we'll soon have more and more people following us and following the vision God gives us. We have to make a shift from being a premature thinking generation to being patient people who don't leave those around us in the dust. You and I will never lead ourselves, our family, or our organization to a God-sized vision if we're too busy hitting the accelerator to think about making sure everyone gets to the destination.

Patience with People

As we have talked about throughout this book, leadership is about people. If we think we're leading but we're ignoring people or using people along the way, we're fooling ourselves. People are why we do what we do. People are the bottom line when it comes to leading anything. If we don't take care of the people we lead, we'll never take care of the goals we set out to achieve. We have to be patient. The people you work with, the people you work for, the people you lead, the people you mentor, the people who mentor you, the people you know, and the people you don't know, all of them mess up. It happened thousands of years ago and it continues to happen today. People will fail. People will stab you in the back. People will be immoral. People will let you down. You and I have to learn to be patient with all of them. Now, don't get me wrong, there's always room for discipline and correction, but be sure patience is practiced on your part as well.

> YOU AND I WILL never lead ourselves, our family, or our organization to a God-sized vision if we're too busy hitting the accelerator to think about making sure everyone gets to the destination.

Why do we have to be patient with those flawed and messed-up people around us? Simply put, you and I are as messed up as them. We're just as messed up, but Jesus was willing to forgive us. Jesus was willing to lead the way and set the example in forgiveness and patience when someone makes a mistake. He knew we would mess up, and He still paid the price. God knew what He was doing when He sent Jesus. He knew some serious grace was needed for you and me. Deuteronomy 31:6 says, "Be strong and courageous. Do not be afraid or terrified because of them, for the Lord your God goes with you; he will never leave you nor forsake you." God promised to never leave or forsake the Israelites in Deuteronomy 31 despite how many times they had abandoned Him during their wandering; He makes the same promise to you. God won't leave you. God forgives you. Forgive others. Be patient with them.

Patience Is Persistent

One of the toughest parts of shifting from premature to patient is that patience is something we have to practice over and over. Patience is one of those things we have to practice with consistency. You see, patience with someone or a project you're in charge of isn't something you can do today and then give up tomorrow. You and I have to be patient each day with it until it's completed. Patience is a grind that has to be done with consistency.

As I've mentioned before, I am something of a runner. Not really because running is a lot of fun to me, more because running is one of those exercises that makes me feel like I'm accomplishing something—at least I'm getting somewhere. Every day when I run, I take a right out of my short driveway and head down a pretty steep hill before continuing on my run. Going downhill when leaving my house isn't that big of a deal. My legs are fresh when I start, my momentum gets me moving down the hill, and I breeze through that first quarter of a mile or so out of my driveway. The problem comes in when I'm on my way home after running four or five miles. By that point, my legs have some pain and my breath is a little short. By the time I'm coming back home, I'm tired and I have to head uphill.

Every time I run, on the last leg, I concentrate on my mailbox. As I head toward my home, the mailbox is my goal, no matter how tired I am or how tough or how steep the stinking hill feels. I concentrate on that mailbox until I get to it and can begin walking and cooling down.

Patience is a lot like running back up that hill near my house.

Patience requires us to be persistent and stay the course. As we make the shift to patience, we'll begin to notice that when we're patient, we stay on course regardless of the setbacks and the hills. When we're persistent in staying the course of patience, we'll recognize the benefits when we get to the end. The mailbox will be worth the patient trek.

Patience Grows

Galatians 5:22–23 says, "But the Holy Spirit produces this kind of fruit in our lives: love, joy, peace, patience, kindness, goodness, faithfulness, gentleness, and self-control. There is no law against these things!" (NLT). Why does the book of Galatians refer to the things in that list as fruit? It calls them fruit because they can grow. You see, the Holy Spirit delivers some level of each of those things in our lives when we become a believer in Christ, but we have to take advantage of the opportunities God gives us to grow those things over time. If you're not perfect at being kind or you're not perfect at loving, the good news is you can grow to do those things better. You can grow in patience as well. In fact, for young people and for all leaders, it is a necessity. I'm so glad the amount of patience I had five years ago isn't the same as I have today. I've grown in it. Each time I discover the benefits of being patient, I get a little better at it. Every time I taste the reward of waiting in the pretzel line at the mall, I find myself doing it a little easier the next time. Each time I see someone I was patient with have the lightbulb of self-discovery go off in their head, I'm able to be a little more patient to the next person. Each time I exercise patience in accomplishing a long-term project and see the project accomplish its purpose in the end, I'm a little more patient next time. Just as we grow in stature, we can grow in patience.

MAKING THE SHIFT

If patience is to grow inside of each of us, we have to have the ability to exercise it. We have to begin making the shift from premature to patient now if we're going to be better at it later.

Look for Opportunities

This may seem obvious, but if we're going to make the shift from premature and grow in patience, we're going to have to look for opportunities to exercise our patience. Stop while you're waiting in line and think about the benefits of waiting in line. Stop when someone disappoints or frustrates you, and focus on love and consider your patience level. It's not just enough to grit our teeth and bear it while waiting. We have to recognize what we're doing so we can know what it's like to improve on it.

Pray Through It

As much as patience is a leadership tool, it's also a spiritual tool. God wants you to be a patient person because He knows the benefits to you and others if you learn to show patience. God understands that, if we'll be patient with our family, we'll raise spiritual giants as kids. God knows if you're patient with an employee, they could be your next department head. God understands if you learn to wait patiently, you'll solve some of your anger issues. When you're in the middle of the shift from premature to patience, it may not seem worth it. Immediate gratification may seem better. Pray through it. Pray through that project that you're losing patience for. Pray through dealing with the difficult person you're leading. Pray through it, and see your patience level shift.

SHIFT SHAPERS

To make the shift from premature to patient, you have to believe . . .

1. Patience is a challenge for us, but it's worth it if we'll make the shift.
2. We are as messed up as the people we lose patience for. Give them another chance.
3. We'll see the rewards at the finish line if we're patient enough to stay in the race.

Patience is persistent. We have to remind ourselves that the destination is worth the process. #NextUpBook

MAKE THE
SHIFT AND GO

We all have those monumental times in life that take us to new places. Not just new places as leaders, but new places as people. For men, those moments are probably a little different than for women. For guys, getting a driver's license, going on a first date, and owning a first car really stand out as big moments while we're growing up. Once we're grown, those defining moments get fewer and further between, but carry a lot more weight and come with a lot more responsibility. Aside from getting married, my biggest moment as a man was when Melissa and I bought our first house.

My wife and I bought our very first home in 2012. Before that, we lived in a parsonage, followed by an apartment we lived in until we were ready to make our big purchase. I vividly remember the search for a house. We were looking for something very specific when it came to our first home. We wanted a home in a certain price range, in a few select locations, and with certain features. We looked at more houses in our small city than I care to remember. Finally, after seeing what seemed like half the houses in our county, we came to the realization that, if we were ever going to actually buy a house, we couldn't look for the perfect house. If we were going to buy a house that met most of our expectations, we were going to have to buy the best available option and start making it into our perfect house.

Since moving into the house we finally chose, we've made some changes. We've bought new furniture, torn down wallpaper, repainted rooms, and done some landscaping along the way. When we first moved into our house, there were three large bushes right in front of the porch. The bushes were so big you could barely see the porch from the road that runs close to the front of our house. About three months into our stay in the house, my wife and I took a Saturday afternoon and cut the bushes down and started to dig them up. I think I still have scars from the blisters on my hands that came from digging and pulling at the roots of those bushes.

You see, the lesson my first home-buying experience taught me was that sometimes you just have to start and not wait for the perfect time. As you've been reading this book, you may be thinking, "I'll never get all of this down. There's no way I can be a *next up* leader." To that thought, I'd say you just have to start. Just start shifting. You won't be perfect overnight. You won't find your dream leadership traits right off the bat. You just have to start shifting and change a little along the way. After all, isn't that the way God works in our lives? Doesn't God offer patience with us and our flaws?

WHEN IT'S TIME TO TAKE YOUR PLACE

One of the greatest examples of the leadership torch being passed is the transition the Israelites went through when their leader Moses died. Moses had been their leader for a long time. Moses led the Israelites through a lot of battles, triumphs, and mistakes. Moses was God's voice, telling Pharaoh to let his people go. Moses gave the Israelites' the Ten Commandments. Moses interceded on the Israelites behalf when God made the decision to wipe them out. Moses led the Israelites through literal troubled waters. Moses was God's mouthpiece to His chosen people.

Moses, though, never saw the Promised Land. Instead, Moses led the people right up to the edge and was forced to pass the torch to God's next chosen man, Joshua.

In Joshua 1, we get a glimpse of the very moment that Joshua took his spot as the *next up* leader of the Israelites. Joshua 1:1–6 says,

> After the death of Moses the servant of the Lord, the Lord said to Joshua son of Nun, Moses' aide: "Moses my servant is dead. Now then, you and all these people, get ready to cross the Jordan River into the land I am about to give to them—to the Israelites. I will give you every place where you set your foot, as I promised Moses. Your territory will extend from the desert to Lebanon, and from the great river, the Euphrates—all the Hittite country—to the Mediterranean Sea in the west. No one will be able to stand against you all the days of your life. As I was with Moses, so I will be with you; I will never leave you nor forsake you. Be strong and courageous, because you will lead these people to inherit the land I swore to their ancestors to give them."

You and I, as *next up* leaders, can learn so much from those verses of Scripture. We can learn so much from Joshua. You see, Joshua wasn't perfect, but he was shifting while Moses was alive. When Moses' life came to an end, Joshua was ready. He was ready to take the baton. The mission was crucial. Joshua would take on leadership over the most loved people of God. Not only that, Joshua was given the opportunity to do what Moses had been leading the people to do for over forty years before . . . take the Promised Land.

ARE YOU WILLING?

When the time comes for you and me to take our place in our organizations, churches, and non-profits, we have to accept that place the same way Joshua did. We have to be humble, strong, and courageous. Joshua modeled humility the entire time he followed Moses. Never once did Joshua overthrow Moses' leadership or try to speak against him. That's why God could tell Joshua to be strong and courageous. God knew that Joshua would take the Israelites to the right place. He knew the people would follow.

The truth is: you have so much to offer. You have a world of potential inside of you. Once you begin making the necessary shifts to utilize that potential, you can begin to walk in the boldness and courage God instructed Joshua to walk in. Once you begin shifting and moving into the place God has called you to, you can begin to see the promised place God has for you.

Jeremiah 1:5 gives all of us some great encouragement as we begin to make the shift in our lives and leadership when it says,

> **IDEAS WILL never matter where movement doesn't take place.**

"*Before* I formed you in the womb I knew you, *before* you were born I set you apart; I appointed you as a prophet to the nations" (emphasis mine). At the time of writing this, my wife is pregnant with our first child. As I sit and pray for my wife and our future son, I can't help but think of all the potential that lies inside of him. I can't help but think of the life he will lead and the things he will see and accomplish. It's unimaginable what our son will go through and make happen. It's unimaginable for me. God already knows it all. He already knows everything about my son's life before his birth. The same can be said of you. God knows where you're going. God knows the leadership potential inside of you. God knows what you'll help accomplish. God knows the frustrations you'll go through and the victories you'll take part in. God knows the progress you'll make, the people you'll reach, and the victories you'll lead. He knows your leadership future. He's called you. It's time to make the shift. It's time to stop waiting for the perfect moment or scenario and just start moving. It's time to quit merely having ideas and dreams and start acting on those. Ideas will never matter where movement doesn't take place.

Start moving.
Start shifting.

The time is now.

NOTES

1. www.merriam-webster.com/dictionary/honor.
2. www.merriam-webster.com/dictionary/premature.

DEDICATION & ACKNOWLEDGMENTS

This book is dedicated first and foremost to God, who makes all things possible and valuable including you and me.

To my wife, Melissa. You are the most precious thing in this world to me. Thank you for putting up with a slightly high-strung and selfish person. Your support helps make everything I do possible. I love you.

To my parents. Thank you for teaching me to love God and others. Thank you for believing in me then, now, and forever. I could not have asked for more loving, sacrificial, and supportive parents. You have instilled great leadership lessons in me because you've always led me well. I love you.

To my brother. I admire you so much, David. Thanks for helping show me the way in life and ministry. So many of these ideas were learned from your example. I'm forever thankful. I love you.

To my extended family. Thank you for your support and helping me become who I am today.

To Artie Davis. Thanks for giving me a chance. Thanks for understanding what's next. Your trust in me has helped more than you know. Thanks for letting me lead. I love you.

To my church family and friends. I love you. Thank you for being a voice in my life and allowing me to be one in yours as well. It's an honor to know you.

To the millennial generation. We have a lot of work to do. We are called to a great task, but we are also called by a great God. We aren't worthy, but we're honored.

Moody Collective brings words of life to a generation seeking deeper faith. We are a part of Moody Publishers, representing this next generation of followers of Christ through books, blogs, essays, and more.

We seek to know, love, and serve the millennial generation with grace and humility. Each of our books is intended to challenge and encourage our readers as they pursue God. To learn more, visit our website, www.moodycollective.com.

www.MoodyPublishers.com

MOODYRADIO

Where you turn. For life.

Moody Radio produces and delivers compelling programs filled with biblical insights and creative expressions of faith that help you take the next step in your relationship with Christ.

You can hear Moody Radio on 36 stations and more than 1,500 radio outlets across the U.S. and Canada. Or listen on your smartphone with the Moody Radio app!

www.moodyradio.org